My CRAZY
summer a memoir

Michael,
Thanks for your
support.
May you see
The hope in
my story.
Continue to
be The difference.
Elaine

My CRAZY
summer a memoir

God, medication, and me...

The Real English Elaine

Xulon Press

Xulon Press
2301 Lucien Way #415
Maitland, FL 32751
407.339.4217
www.xulonpress.com

Illustrated by Jennifer Rogers

About the front cover image.
From left to right the images represent #treemha.
The neutral face - looking/acting "normal".
The tearful face - in the deepest darkest pit.
The joyful face - in a much higher place than neutral, spreading joy
and hope.

Edited by Xulon Press

Printed in the United States of America.

ISBN-13: 978-1-6312-9436-5

Dedication

First and foremost, I want to give God all the glory for giving me the strength, courage, and conviction to write this book. You will hear me say later in the book that I would not want even my worst enemy to go through what I went through. However, I wouldn't change the experience for the world. I sincerely believe that God is in the details, and everything happens for a reason.

To my husband Kevin, who is my hero. I thank him for standing by me and being my physical rock. He could have quite easily walked out and given up, but he stuck with me. "Through better or worse, richer or poorer, in sickness or in health," is what he said to me at the start of my crazy summer.

To my wonderful girlfriends — you know who you are. You prayed for me, fasted for me, and even though I blocked out all but one—Christine, I know you were there. Christine, my faithful prayer partner – thank you!

To my company, PwC — without their care and support, it would have been a really tough journey.

It may also seem crazy to thank all the people and events that led me to my crazy summer. I have forgiven each one of you. I thank you for leading me to an experience that has given me a deeper sense of who I am and what my purpose is.

Lastly, to everyone out there who is experiencing mental illness and think that suicide is the only option. I'm living proof that there is hope. In Part 5, I have included excerpts from the journal I wrote at the time, so you can see how crazy my thoughts were. Maybe you can relate.

My prayer is that if this book helps one person, then my mission to publish this book is complete.

Remember, you may have "crazy" times. However, through it all, "God is crazy about you."

Table of Contents

Preface

I know my story is not unique, because of the increased awareness of mental health issues. I also know I am not professionally qualified to give advice on medication. What worked for me may not work for you. There are many different levels of depression; some require medication, others do not – counselling may be the answer.

Someone recently shared an analogy with me I think is pretty sound. Most people get a cold and can handle it. However, if you get pneumonia, then you need to seek professional help. I think this applies to mental health issues also. Many people experience different levels of stress, even panic attacks, that they are able to deal with. However, when the episodes get out of control and impact your way of life, and the lives of those around you, then you need to seek professional help. Makes sense, right?

I am not a doctor, so I asked my current, wonderful doctor to provide some medical guidance, that way I do not unwittingly cause someone to do something harmful.

Message from doctor

Thanks, Elaine, for giving me this important opportunity. For the readers, I am Dr. Anielka Rodriguez.

I have been Elaine's primary care physician for the past five years. I appreciate Elaine's real honesty about her story, and I'm convinced it may help others understand the intricacies and tensions around mental health and its different ways to treat it including, as in her particular case, the requirement of using medication.

As a medical professional, it is my duty and responsibility to offer a disclaimer: The information in this book is not intended to be in any way an explicit or implied substitute for professional medical advice. If you identify in any way with Elaine's story, YOU MUST SEEK MEDICAL COUNSEL FOR PROPER DIAGNOSIS AND TREATMENT. Please do not use this book as a tool to self-diagnose, as it is NOT its purpose to serve as a replacement for medical advice or treatment. If you have any questions, please reach out to your doctor.

May you be encouraged by this memoir.

Stop and read before you move on

You may be reading this page – online, in a bookstore, at an airport - you may be in different places with many different things going through your mind.

There is a reason the title captured your attention:

1. Are you going through your own "crazy summer"?
2. Are you a family member/friend of someone going through a crazy summer?
3. Have you been through a crazy summer experience and can relate to my story?
4. Or, are you simply browsing and curious about what this book is all about?

Whatever the reason, you are reading this page. I want to invite you to flip through—maybe some pages will speak more to you than others.

You will see many references to God, Jesus Christ, and Christianity. I don't know what tradition is at the foundation of your faith. I do want to encourage you that whatever it is, if it is different than mine, don't let this stop you from reading further. Remember, this is my story. Yours is likely to be different. The purpose of this book is to be part of the movement of raising awareness on the topic of mental and emotional health.

#treemha (therealenglishelainementalhealthawareness) #stigmafree (linked to NAMI.org)

Please don't be put off or offended by the Christian references; I'm assuming positive intent. This is a memoir, my story.

I do have a specific message if you are from the faith-based community and reading this. There seems to be a challenge in "the church" whenever the topic of medication comes up. As the subtitle of my book states, I believe in some cases you need both faith and medicine. God provides people with talents and gifts. The medical community are placed in our path to provide the specialist help and support that is needed when our "little panic attack," or "feelings of I'm so stressed" reach a point where they impact not only your life but those around you.

Whatever the reason you picked up this book, you picked it up. Are you ready to take a deep breath, have an open mind and heart, remove your filters and biases, and come along on this journey with me? If so, read on.

My memoir is split into different parts to help you, the reader, navigate the pages.

Setting the scene gives a high level overview of the story before diving into the details.

Part 1 – the events and triggers that lead up to my crazy summer

Part 2 – The crazy summer in detail. From me trying to attempt suicide to the time spent in the difference places where help was provided.

Part 3 – The power of support. The importance of staying in community and not isolating.

Part 4 and 4a – What life is like now.

Part 5 – Journal entries. In full transparency and vulnerability, I share the journal I kept during my crazy summer. It is kept true to form so that you are able to see how the text changes in so many ways. This gives insight to what could be going on in the mind of someone who has seemingly "got it all together" on the outside.

Songs - I finish with sharing some of the many songs that influenced me and continue to do so. Maybe you will find encouragement from the lyrics.

As I came to the end of writing this book, I realized there was so much more to share. Therefore, instead of one book, this is the first in a trilogy. Yup, I never thought I could write one book, and now I am in the process of brainstorming books 2 and 3.

I already have the titles:

Book 2: The Real English Elaine: Stranger Connections

Book 3: The Real English Elaine: Faithfully Healthy

Watch this space!

Setting the scene

Sunday May 17, 2015: I stood in front of my home church at that time, Steele Creek Church in Charlotte, North Carolina, where my family and I had been attending for more than ten years, and the place where we were "saved."

What follows is my testimony, which sets the stage for the rest of the book in which you see my testimony in detail and being expanded.

Let me set some context for my testimony. This would be the final time we would attend our home church in North Carolina, as we were moving to Central Florida soon. The weekend was significant, not only because we were leaving our church but because it was also a year since I started my "crazy summer." I wanted to use this opportunity to stand in front of the church (at both services) to share that we are all vulnerable, and even when we may feel there is no hope, there is.

Testimony at Church-May 17, 2015

I want to start off by saying our God is amazing, and I give Him all the glory. He is so in the details, and many times it is not until we look back that we see His hand at work. That's why history is His-story. For those of you who don't know me, I'm Elaine. My husband Kevin and I have been coming to this church for more than ten years.

We were both saved at this church, and I thank God for using Pastor Dale Shields, who was a guest preacher that day. I got saved in the "big tent" before the sanctuary was built.

I come from a Catholic background, so when friends invited us to a non-denominational church, we went, both because we were curious and to please our friends. (Note to self: Never give up on inviting people.)

When we arrived, I was totally freaked out. People were hugging us, there was free coffee and tea. I was thinking, "Where was the order of service?" People were clapping, raising their hands, shouting out. They were telling us God had spoken to them and told them what to do! I asked Kevin in the car, "What does God sound like? Is it a big boom-boom voice?" Now I know that many times He speaks in a quiet, gentle whisper.

As far as raising hands and singing, now I gladly and thankfully raise my hands. I recall the first time I did this, I felt urged by the Holy Spirit (I didn't know that at the time). I tentatively raised my hands. Often, I would be wondering who was looking at me and what were they thinking. Now I know it's between me and God. I boldly and gladly raise my hands, and sing and shout for all that He has done for me.

When I got saved, I recall the feeling of freedom, and the weight of sin and guilt leaving me. I cried and cried. When the "altar call" was made, I got up and walked to the front. As I returned to my seat, a friend asked me if I had accepted Jesus into my heart. First thought I had was, "Have I joined a cult?"

Now I know I have become in union with the one and only true God, and there are no rules like I had in the Catholic religion. It's simply a matter of repenting of sin and asking Jesus into your heart. You then enter into a personal relationship with God, which is the best relationship in the world.

Being saved doesn't mean that life becomes easier. In fact, it can become harder. Apostle James tells us that **when** we have trials, not **if,** we are to count it all a joy. I have the faith to know that Christ will walk with me through it. (Added second service. You may be thinking, "Glad I don't know Christ…my life is very comfortable, and I have all I need and can do all that I want with no consequences." Sadly, if you don't know Christ, life may seem "perfect" on this side of heaven. That is because Satan already has you. You have not committed your life to Christ, so why would he try to fight to get you back?)

Remember we are here for a brief moment, and we are taken away in the blink of an eye. I would rather live here going through life with the peace and joy of Christ inside me, knowing that I will live with Him forever in eternity. You are either for God or against Him – you can't be in the middle, lukewarm. (Rev. 3:15-16 - I know your deeds, that you are neither cold nor hot. I wish you were either one or the other! So, because you are lukewarm—neither hot nor cold—I am about to spit you out of my mouth.) However, there is hope, as He loves all and wants all to come to Him. No matter how you think or feel about God/Christ now, He is always there, ready for you.

It has been quite a journey, and I wanted to share that this weekend is very significant not just because we are being honored to have the church pray for us, as we get ready to move to Florida. It has been exactly one year since May 16 2014, when I called my boss to quit my job. Thankfully, my boss talked me off the ledge and told me I should take some time to get help – 5-7 weeks, whatever I needed. That was the start of an almost six-month journey, in which at one point I tried to end my life with pills, ended up in a psych unit for ten days, and a patient in an outpatient program for three weeks.

I was in a severe depression, one in which I thought God had forsaken me. I was reaching out, reading the Bible, but all I saw was the negative. I was the rich young ruler, the seed in the thorn bush. Thankfully, my husband would rebuke the lies. Whenever I said that God had left me, he would simply respond with, "No, He hasn't." Whenever I thought I had lost my salvation, my best friend would remind me I can't lose my salvation.

My doctors were telling me I needed medication, which I was against. I had well-meaning people make me question my belief and advised against medication. I clearly had a chemical imbalance; it was not a faith issue. My God is faithful. Now I take one small dose daily, and with God, I continue to pray I will be used for His glory. Think about it. If you have a broken leg, you need to see a doctor. I totally believe miracles can happen; however, I also believe, in the West, we block many of the miracles because we try to take God's place.

In a church this size, I can only imagine there is at least one person going through what I was. Or there is one person who is thinking about taking a step of faith to give his or her life to Christ. If you are that person, all I can do is encourage you. Take the step. When you do, you are guaranteed eternity with Jesus. However, what's more exciting to me is having the joy and peace of living with Jesus while you are here through the journey. Some people have told me that is a decision they will make on their death bed. My response is a question: "How do you know when you are going to be on your death bed?" We could walk out of here today and lose our lives in a million different ways. We are not guaranteed tomorrow.

As we get ready to leave this church building, but not the Church, I want to take the opportunity to thank God for His grace and peace. I thank my husband, Kevin, for sticking with me throughout this time and reminding me of our wedding vows, "for better or worse, richer or poorer, in sickness and in health." For my best friend, Christine, who has been my faithful prayer partner for the last ten years: She walked with me last year and got all my friends together to pray and fast for me. I only found that out a few months ago. If you are not plugged into the church, I would encourage you to make a connection. There is power in community.

God continues to work in the details. We met a Christian lady at a coffee shop in Florida, whose mother's house we ended up buying. The mother is widowed and want to use the money to do mission work. We already have found an amazing church called Real Life.

Please continue to keep us in prayer. Satan is not happy and will continue to attack. I share my story to bring truth to light.

We will continue to keep you in prayer. God bless.

When I gave this testimony, at the end of each service, I was encouraged by the number of people who came up. Some of them were surprised because they never knew what I was going through. They thought I had "it all" and I was so "put together." My only response can be, "I'm human, and because of this, I'm not perfect and we all struggle."

The rest of this book goes into more details surrounding this testimony and my "crazy summer." I choose not to continue to live in the darkness and experience the shame surrounded by someone who attempted suicide. Instead, I want to share my story to give hope and bring light to darkness.

You have picked up this book for a reason. My prayer is that as you read it, you have an open mind and heart. If you do know Christ, my prayer is that you experience peace and joy that transcends all understanding, and you have the courage to be the light on the hill and bring light to darkness.

PART I –
Events and Triggers

Many times, what leads you to the place of darkness, which feels like the deepest valley, the very pit of hell, is really a series of events happening over a period of time. Then, while in the valley, one experience is the "straw that breaks the camel's back." You are tipped over the edge into a place where you feel so overwhelmed and out of control that you really need help.

When you get through the valley, on the other side, you look back and many times you can say, "Now, I know why I went through this." I once heard someone say, "God uses our messes to create the message." This is true in my case.

In this section, I share some of the significant events, the triggers, that led to my crazy summer. Between them, I can imagine there were many small events/triggers that contributed.

Where do I begin? When did this all start? Probably a very long time ago, but the summer of 2014 was when it took me to the pit of hell and, thankfully, my dear Lord did not leave me or forsake me (as much as I thought He had.)

2007 – 2009: Let Go and Let God

What a difference a day makes: I had written this in my Grace Life Advance Discipleship paper in 2009. The title of the paper was "Let Go and Let God." How could I have ever imagined that someone in an outpatient psychiatric unit would be saying the same words to me five years later?

My final paper was all about the fact that I had surrendered my life to God. I realized I am not in control; only He is and when I rest in that truth, I have a peace that surpasses all understanding. Of course, I'm human and live in a fallen world, so there are many times I forget this and try to take control back. Five years ago, I had let go of my job, my finances, and my daughter. I still recall in the paper I commented on the fact that I had not let my husband go and I still tried to control him.

What follows is my Grace Life "Let go and let God" paper.

Have you felt like you are the square peg in a round hole? (As I sit on a plane in 2019, reviewing my book, I am reminded that I recently used this exact phrase to someone else!) Have you ever wondered what this is all about? Have you ever said "Really Lord, what is this all about?" Have you felt like saying to yourself, *Lord I can't do this anymore*, or *Why have you put me here?* Have you had the feeling of waking up, with a pit in your stomach, and going into the bathroom, shouting "*I can't do this anymore*"?

I have worked all my life with a performance-based mentality. I just have to work, work, work. I believed the lie that I was not good enough, not worthy enough. Because of my poor background, I was not meant to have "a good life." I didn't have work/life balance and didn't spend time with my family. (Fast forward to 2019. I prefer to use the phrase: Life balance. Work is part of your life, not separate from it. There is an entire movement that speaks to the philosophy, which I agree with, that we need to bring our whole selves to work: physical, mental, emotional, and spiritual.)

The Lord took me away from all that and brought me to America from England. Once again, I continued to work out of my own strength, because I did not know any better. I thought if I did a good job, people would think I am good enough. The problem was I never felt good enough, so I continued to work. Have you ever felt that way and woken up one morning to wonder what it's all about?

When I started going to my new church, one of the things I would hear people constantly say is, "You just have to let go and let God." Oh, how that can seem such a trite, Christianese saying. How many times have you said it or heard it, and really fully understood the power of the saying? I have said this to a friend so many times.

In the past, one friend asked me, "How do I do that (let go and let God)?"

My response at that time was, "You simply give it to God and He will sort it out."

This is normally followed by a response, "I can't do that."

Which is followed by another "supportive" Christian's response by quoting Philippians 4:13, "I can do all things through Christ who strengthens me."

Yet, as I now understand more of the power of those phrases, my response would be different. If you have truly given your life to the Lord and believe that He died for our sins (1 Cor. 15:3) and that I died with Him (Rom. 7:4 and Gal. 2:20), then shouldn't it be relatively easy to let go and let God? Correct!

It's very hard to separate how we view ourselves in the workplace and the home, and as I have ultimately learned, the issue is that living a victorious Christian life is not about living the life; it really is about understanding who I am. By knowing who I am, I am able to fully and totally surrender myself to the Lord; and, in doing so, receive all the blessings that He has in store for me.

It really is easier "to do" once you "become." It just gets easier to cast all our burdens on Him, the one who cares for you [1 Pet. 5:5,7); if we give up on our self-life and the control, we think we have.

Let me take you on a journey of brokenness and surrender so you can appreciate the joy that can be received from living a victorious Christian life, and understand more about why He has me where He has me.

I first attended Grace Life International (GLI) Advanced Discipleship Training class (ADT) as part of the Fall 2007 class. I was going through yet another tough time my job was changing, my daughter was living in New York, and I seemed to have continued financial issues, even though I thought that by this time in my life I had those conquered.

Before attending class, when my first counselor commented I may be going through depression, I totally disagreed. I was not a candidate for the D word; I was in control and I would not allow myself to be depressed! But, why was it that the same issues in my life seem to recur? What I didn't fully appreciate is that God turns the pressure on all areas of brokenness if we are not prepared to "let go and let God."

In 2007, I had been attending my church for six years. I remember coming to the church and being totally freaked out. (As I testified earlier) I was saved at Steele Creek Church of Charlotte (SCCC), and remember the freedom I felt on the day of salvation. A huge weight was lifted off my shoulders; I fully repented of all my sins, gave my life to the Lord, and asked Him to live in me and take care of my life. What a joyful day. The joy continued as I learned that all my sins were taken away at the cross, as far as the East is from the West. Not only were they my sins of the past, but also the present and the future. In 1 Corinthians 1:30, I knew that I had given up my life to the Lord and I thought that now all I had to do was be a good Christian and He would sort out my life.

Pastor Charles Stanley comments on how we create a circle around us, of what we still want to control (Stanley 1991). We give it all to God, except this little piece. I was always fearful of not having enough money, as I had a poor upbringing and wanted to ensure my family would not be that way. I was the breadwinner, so I controlled how the money was spent. Being saved, I also knew that now I had to financially give to the Lord in the form of tithing.

Sometimes I was really anxious about giving money and did not give my full tithes. (One time I even canceled a check!) In doing so, I now understand I was restricting God's blessings. I was thinking my God was a mighty God, but He wasn't big enough to take me through this tough time.

The Lord convicted me, through my husband, and we attended a Crown Financial Ministries class where I learned the importance of giving with a cheerful heart (2 Cor. 9:7). Also, I now know I didn't have to give; it's about giving with the right heart attitude. This reminds me that obedience of faith brings about the peace God desires for me.

I prayed Psalm 139:23: "Search me oh God and know my heart; test me and know my anxious thoughts." I want the Lord to show me my heart attitude, but what is the motive for me doing this?' I thought, *Is it to get my needs met or is it the godly thing to do?* I gave control of my finances to the Lord. I know that He is my provider, Jehovah Jireh, and it is amazing how the Lord has shown up in the area of finances. It's so true that we reap what we sow (Gal. 6:7.)

The Lord appeared not just in material things, but in the joy of being able to assist others. There is a peace that comes with knowing I cannot be anxious about tomorrow, because we are only guaranteed today, (Matt. 6:34.) He continues to show up in so many ways—I have so many God stories in this area of finance. So, I had given my finances for the Lord, but I continued to keep my daughter and my job in my circle of control.

My daughter Angela was off at college and living in New York. I was still trying a long-distance control relationship with her. I was the one that had given her everything; the one that had managed to get her where she was. I wanted her to be successful and had such huge expectations for her. In order for her to be successful, of course I had to control as much as I could. So many times, I had given her to God, but so many times I had taken her back.

It was during a one-on-one conversation with the Lord I heard Him tell me to trust Him and be anxious for nothing (Phil. 4:6.) "Oh, but you don't know how hard this is Lord. She is my baby, my one and only child; how could I do this?" Of course, I could not do it; it is through Christ's strength living in me that I was able to totally surrender her to the Lord. I had the faith of Abraham being prepared to sacrifice Isaac.

I knew I could not do it, yet I truly had to let go and let God. It was painful, and also painful to see her journey unfold. The praise is that it was so pleasing to hear her say the following words to me after she returned home from living in New York.

"Mum, you know that you said that you had changed since you had become a Christian, but living in New York, I could not see that. Now living back home, I can see that you have changed, and that you are a lot less controlling than you have been in the past."

Praise God! What an affirmation. On Mother's Day, she presented me with a homemade card – she knows I prefer this to the Hallmark card. Inside, she had written: "Mum, I know the last twenty-five years have been bumpy, but the next twenty-five will be wonderful. I love you and like you."

As a child, she would often tell me she didn't like me! My continued prayer for her is that she grows in Christ and continues to experience the joy and freedom from simply being and not doing.

My Christianese response now to Angela is it's, "between you and God." Because at the end of the day, that actually is all that matters. One day, you're going to be present at the judgment seat of Christ and have to give an account of your actions (2 Cor. 5:9,10.) It has been a joy to see Christ work in her heart.

I wish I could say that our relationship is all perfect. By contrast, there have been times my flesh has risen up in certain situations and I have made flesh choices with Angela. The outcome from these has never been great; however, I rest in knowing that I can repent, confess my sins, and enjoy the Lord's presence.

I was still continuing in my cycle of co-dependency, looking in particular to my husband and job to get my worth. Remember I had given my daughter to the Lord, so I was not as dependent on her anymore to get my basic Love Acceptance, Worth, and Security (LAWS) needs met. I was continuing to do, rather than be, and I was still in a cycle of seeking acceptance by performing.

It was through history-taking process at ADT I came to understand: A) my mixed flesh. I was a negatively-programmed person who looked positive; B) The impact of the messages given to me by my upbringing and the beliefs I had about myself being unworthy; C) That my father had a huge impact and affected how I view God; D) My need to control and perform as being coping mechanisms for life, both at work and at home.

I began to overcome my fleshly needs for performance-based acceptance. I needed to overcome this, but I could not; it can only be done by Christ who lives in me (Col. 3:10.)

I knew in my head that I am complete in Christ, and He is my all. So why was it at the beginning of 2009, I had to once again deal with control of my job. It's amazing what a difference a day makes, and in a matter of a day, my job world had turned upside down. The economic downturn had hit, and since I had left college, I had always worked and wanted to continue to provide. I was in a position to decide whether to work for the company that gave me business or go independent and be totally on my own? Oh, how I wrestled with this, reminding me of Jacob and God. For almost three months, I thought I heard from the Lord, and yet I had slipped into depression once again, even admitting it this time.

When I was not working, I was sleeping. At one stage, I contemplated walking onto my deck at my house and throwing myself over. It was not high enough; I would just break a leg: I also knew in my heart the thoughts were coming from Satan. I chose to take those thoughts captive. Did anyone notice a change in me? Could they see my depression? Probably not, because my flesh was great at creating a mask.

I bound the spirit of depression, stood on my authority of sitting at the right hand of Christ. Yet, it took some time for the feelings to catch up with my belief. Now, I do feel peace. What I have to come to learn, know, and believe is that I need to lose my life (John 12:24) in order to gain eternal life—Christ life—and in doing so, rest in knowing that I will continue to go through the brokenness process, which I should count as a joy (James 1) while going through the trials. The real joy is in knowing who I am in Christ. God loves me not because of who I am, but because of who He is. I not only learned that, but fully understood with all my heart I am complete in Christ and don't need anyone else.

I have learned to love myself and understand I can't love others until I love myself. In counseling, this was a big breakthrough. My counselor asked me, "Do you love yourself?"

In my heart I knew that I did not, but I would never have admitted that. However, what did I gain by lying to my counselor? Why give Satan one more victory? So, I honestly responded, "No, I don't." In fact, I hated myself for all the horrible, fleshy stuff that I was holding onto: my thoughts and the way I treated my daughter, husband, and job. I wanted to control and was afraid that if "it" (it being anything) did not go my way, there was a fear of rejection. I had to truly let that go and accept that my identity is in Christ, and He is where I can get my LAWS needs met. That it truly is not about me.

This doesn't mean I've become passive and said, "Ok Lord, I give it all up to You; You take over." It's about having Christ living within me and through me. He wants to use Elaine for His glory. I learned I had to accept God's love for me before I could truly love others. This is grounded in my identity with Christ (Gal. 2:20) so that I can fulfill a commandment (2 John 13:34) to love one another as I have loved you; in giving control to God and doing what He says (Phil. 2:5,7).

I had to forgive myself first before I could forgive others. I repented on believing my whole life is built on the structure of performance. Pastor Malcolm Smith states:

> I die to doing and become a being. I believe I am unconditionally loved and I come just as I am. I find my significance in what He says about me, not what I say about me to Him. I understand that brokenness is getting rid of self-life, which does not mean losing my zest for life, walking in the joy of the Lord, in who I am, and all that I say and do.

Maybe there is something in the fact that we are called "human beings," not "human doings." We are called to be, not do.

Pastor Charles Stanley posed this challenge, and I paraphrase: if you want God's blessings, how many of you are willing to allow God to do whatever is necessary to bring you to the position of total surrender, so that He can do all He wants to do and is free to do it? (Stanley 2002) For Christ to break all that is in your life and, all that is within you, for Him to take complete and overwhelming control of your soul?

I don't know how many blessings I've missed because of my controlling spirit. I want the Lord to continue to reveal to me what I am holding onto, so I will not miss God's best for me.

I have not only learned but have also experienced the area of brokenness and fully understand that in order to receive the joy and blessing, I have to be broken and die to myself. How often have I been through brokenness, reached an obstacle, and said, "I know I can't do that," "I know that could not happen," especially with my job. Why do I think that I'm not good enough, not worthy enough for God's blessings? I don't need to live a poor, lowly, lonely life. The Christian life is joyful, and I am to be thankful in all circumstances (1 Thess. 5:18) and be anxious for nothing (Phil. 4:6)

There are so many great analogies that can be used about how God shapes us: we are the pottery made by the potter's hands; the chisel used by the sculptor; in order to make wine or juice, the grape has to be crushed; in order for the field to yield a harvest of wheat, a dead seed needs to be buried to bring about the harvest.

I think many of the analogies can be summarized by secular sayings I have shared for many years, and yet only recently begun to fully understand the significance, "Short-term loss, long-term gain." Dying now to self in the short term, I am going to reap huge rewards, which I have already started to receive and for the long term —eternity. I don't want to miss out on God's design for my life.

Every area of my life is now brought into submission to God. My life is to be an indwelling expression of Christ. As I say the words, "Lord, I'm waiting for You to break any aspect of my life, no matter what it is, in order to prepare me to become the total person that You created me to be," it kind of makes my stomach sick; this is because I know there are things I would hate to lose. But who says I will lose them? I'm simply giving up my rights to keep them.

I want to achieve the work in this world that He wants me to achieve. I am prepared to rest in Him, so that He can do His work in me. I believe that what God has for me is better than I ever can imagine. I'm stepping out and trusting what God will give me.

One of my favourite verses, posted in my house, is very familiar— (Prov. 3:4, 6.) I love the version from the Message:

Trust God from the bottom of your heart; don't try to figure out everything on your own. Listen for God's voice in everything you do, everywhere you go; He's the one who will keep you on track. Don't assume that you know all.

I know with all my heart, mind, and soul I cannot live the Christian life and be in the workplace with God's help because He is not helping me; He is doing it through me.

I said at the beginning that I wanted to take on a journey. This really is a journey, and the final destination is your heavenly home. I most certainly have not arrived to yet.

Whilst on this earth, I desire to live a surrendered life. In order to do this, I need to die daily (1 Cor. 15:31) and give up all my rights. This is a daily choice. I wake up in the morning and my first thought is on Christ, that the day is His and that He is to guide all my thoughts, words, and actions. People are able to see Him in me, so I want my life to be used for His glory. You will never know whose lives you touch in the workplace. You are the light in the darkness. There have been times when people have looked at me and thought I was crazy—the only answer I had was "It's God."

When I was working for my previous company, and they were down-sizing, I was going through the green card process. I could not lose my job or I would have to go back to England. I knew God was in control. People wondered why I was not anxious! I was given my notice on one project; the following Friday I was moved to another part of the company; and the next Friday I was notified about my green card, the next Friday I received my green card. Four consecutive Fridays: now tell me that's not God.

I continue to be in awe of Him. I'm not sure why, because He is awesome. He is so in the details. Just take a moment to think how He has shown up and continues to show up in our lives. When you are in the office and you want time to get the project complete, and something happens and you get the time, that's God.

I want to conclude by sharing with you an excerpt from "He Loves Me" by Wayne Jacobsen (1995):

Father, may the purpose for which you created me and placed me where you have in the world to be fulfilled completely. This prayer disarms all self-interest and asserts all trust that the father made us and who loves us so deeply that he knows us better than ourselves.

He continues:

> We have two choices we can pray Father save me, or Father glorify your name. Choose to save yourself and you will find yourself resisting God when you don't even mean to. You will end up praying against the very things God is using to transform you or the ways He rescued you. You will miss Him because they won't look like the things you want. (Jacobsen 2007)

I know the Christ life is my identity and not my job. My job will come and go, but He is always there. Although total surrender is an act of giving control over to God, it is also the greatest act of receiving the finished work of the cross, personally for one's self. You're working out His strengths and not yours. The cross is not so that God could love me; it is so that I can love Him. I received the truth and reality of Christ living His life through me. I choose to receive and believe that I am worthy, I am acceptable, I am lovable, I am a saint, and I am the salt of the earth. This leads me to a life of abiding, trusting, faith, and being led into receiving the exchange life (Isa. 5:3; Isa. 6:1). I know God loves me not because of who I am, but because of who He is. I choose to lean on the Lord and live out of who I am, remembering that it's not about living the Christian life; it is about understanding who I am.

All these thoughts and this growth was in 2011, three years before my major depression episode. Isn't it amazing how we think we have learned and got it altogether, then we become comfortable, complacent, and need another jolt? Another stripping of the coal to reveal the diamond, and another chipping away at the structure to reveal the beauty? This will continue throughout our lives. The hope is that each time we are becoming more mature, and the strike that touched us last time doesn't hurt as much, as we draw closer to our Saviour.

Or, is it that we become more mature and go to a deeper level that we are able to draw closer to our God? Are we learning to truly live in His peace and joy, as we enjoy His presence and keep Him as the focus of our day? I have been reminded so many times that peace is not a state where everything is quiet and there is no noise— true peace is being able to rest and enjoy a peace that surpasses all understanding, in spite of the noise. There is a well-known saying that illustrates this:

Life isn't about waiting for the storm to pass...It's about learning to dance in the rain. (Greene 2013)

2011

Immediately after *Advanced Discipleship Training*, life was a challenge. I am fully aware the more you deepen your relationship with the Lord (because you can't get any closer to Him then you already are), the more you're going to be stretched. The goal is to be refined like the potter molding his clay. This reminds me of the song "Potter's hands" by Hillsong Worship. Funny though how as we go about our daily life, we can easily forget this.

After ADT, I became an independent consultant. I quickly got to work with a small boutique consulting firm. After working there for four years, we were acquired by one of the largest consulting firms in the world! This was a proud moment, and became a huge, personal challenge for me.

People thought I brought so much experience to the table, and yet I doubted myself so much. I thought I was not good enough or smart enough. Sound familiar? How could I possibly compete with all these young twentysomethings who had just come out of top graduate schools with MBA degrees? What I failed to realize is that education was all many of them had. They did not have the battle scars and experience of being in the real world. They had not yet had to manage the responsibility of being a wife, mother, and a friend, as well as trying to please CEOs and CFOs running multimillion, even billion-dollar, firms.

From day one, I was challenged. I was put on a client project immediately, the plastic business. What did I know about plastic business? What I failed to remember is it doesn't matter most what business it is— of course it helps to understand how a business runs and the issues particular to that business—however, that can be learned. What is important is truly the relationships and the people who run the business. I have a gift for connecting with people, and yet when I think it is about the business, I lose perspective.

Here I was with the client in a large firm, dealing with the daily operations of being part of a firm that had many compliance rules. So much structure, process, so many things that had to be done. In the small boutique firm, we focused on people and relationships. We signed a contract and then off we went to deliver. Now there were so many rules, forms that needs to be completed, processes that needed to be followed. I fully understand and appreciate the need for these things—we didn't want to be another Enron. It was just challenging. I put so much pressure on myself to perform, and I can be such a perfectionist. I would have my head in the toilet each morning baulking, not being sick but just feeling very sick! Why was I putting myself through this? Why did I have to go through this? Lord, am I just not good enough or smart enough? Each day I got out of bed, head in the toilet, would pull myself together, and then off to work I would go to perform.

I had a great leader at the time who was there for me. He is a Christian friend, a devout Christian who has a great, deep relationship with the Lord. Many times, he would remind me whose I was, not who I was! Lord, I needed to be reminded of that.

I would finish one project, then because it was successful, I was placed on another, with no downtime. In the meantime, I was still not happy with my place in life, especially at work. One day I walked into a friend's office, another Christian colleague from our small boutique firm. He reminded me that I had so much more than these young people. Not only did I have Christ, I also had my experience. Many people who come to work straight from college simply "follow the playbook." Oftentimes, the situation would change, and the playbook needed to be rewritten on the fly— we had to adapt, which I had plenty of experience doing.

I was still not convinced. I reached out to my prayer partner, who constantly reminded me that we have been in this place before. Each time I start a new role, a new job, I would doubt myself. It's because I think I should have all the answers. How could I possibly have all the answers? One thing I've learned from the people business is that throughout life, we are constantly learning. Life is one big, lifelong learning experience. How could I possibly think I could get by with what I learned several years ago?

Everything is constantly changing, and we must learn to adapt. However, there is one constant—Christ. He is unchanging, and never leaves you or forsakes you. I love that the constant is actually all about relationships and intentionality. As author Maya Angelou wrote:

> *I've learned that people will forget what you said, people will forget what you did, but people will never forget how you made them feel. (Angelou 2003)*

I believe that we have to be Christ to others, to be the light to the world and for others to see what is different; and that the difference is Him living in and through us.

I intellectually know all this; however, life was still horrible for me. Why did I think I needed to have all the answers? Pride! I've been working for twenty-plus years, shouldn't I have all the answers? Will people think I'm weak if I ask the question? I couldn't take it anymore. I thought I needed to leave the company. What could I do that did not require me to be perfect? Something that I would not have to think about? Something that will be easy.

How about working in a coffee shop? I went online to complete an application form. I got to the income section. How could I put down my current salary? They would laugh at me. I decided I couldn't do it; I'd go back to the treadmill of performance-based acceptance, being sick each day.

In the same year, one Christmas my in-laws visited, and I was having a particularly bad spell; such that I would curl up and cry on the floor, talking about how I could not do this anymore. How many times did I use the word "I"? What kind of joy was I demonstrating to my family? Why would anyone want to trust in the Lord when they saw how I was feeling?

I had intellectually known all the right answers to give people. I even gave advice to my friends, as they were going through tough times. My response each time would be to continue to look to Jesus and cast your cares on Him; how He is in total control. How many times have you heard someone say, who knows what is going to happen in the situation and the response given, quite flippantly say, "Who knows? God knows?" Do people truly believe what they say that it is only truly God knows?

So here I am, again, in the place. I decided to speak to somebody who had been with the firm for a while. He gave me some solid advice and reminded me that the firm is a tough place to get into. However, once in, providing you are a good performer, the firm will work with you to find a place for you to be your best. How amazing is that, not something you see often in corporate America; a firm that actually cares for its people. I listened, heard, and decide to continue on.

Over the next few months of becoming more familiar with the situation and accepting where I was, I was reminded after coffee with my

Christian colleague that my identity cannot be found in my work. Work situations will come and go, my identity is forever in Christ.

In my Advanced Discipleship Training class five years ago, I had written, "I am, because He is." I have to remind myself about that constantly. Today, I had a "come to Jesus" meeting with myself and once again accepted that my value, worth, and security does not come from others but from the Lord. My significance is because of Him. I am here for the purpose of glorifying His name and to be His disciple, to draw others to Him. I cannot save anyone; all I can do is sow seeds and hopefully through my actions, I can influence my unsaved family, friends, and colleagues to come to know Christ as their Lord and Savior. Not just to simply fulfill that fire insurance policy so that they can go to heaven and not hell, but also to have the joy and peace of having God living in them through them, whilst they are still alive on earth.

How many times have you thought that you are going down one path, only to find yourself in a totally different place? Does the different place freak you out, or do you find contentment in all circumstances? Do you see God's hand in it at all? He is so in the details when we just take a moment to reflect and see how He has shaped our lives, today, the last hour. Someone once said there are no such things as coincidences, only God-incidences.

I felt in a much better place and had gone back to my Lord. He never leaves us or forsakes us, but we turn our backs on Him. Take a moment to do this simple exercise. Put your hands together like you are getting ready to pray. This is what it is like when we are conscious of the Lord living in us and we are depending on Him. Can you see and feel the two palms of your hands touching each other?

Next, turn **one** of your palms the other way. This palm is you. You now have your back turned on God, but He is still there. He never moves, for we are the ones that move. He is still faithful, waiting for you to come back to Him; like you did the first time you surrendered your life to Him. He is patient and will wait as long as you live to return to Him.

I do believe that once saved, you are saved; you may drift away due to the fact that you and I are all human and live in a fallen world. Even when we are in the pit of hell, or what feels like that way, when we don't see Him or hear Him, He is always there, no matter what. This reminds me of a song "Not for a Moment" by Meredith Andrews, one of my favourite songs of all times. The lyrics tell us about how God is there, even when it doesn't feel like it.

2012

Summer of 2012, I experienced the joy of my daughter's wedding. I was so proud of her, for she has truly blossomed into the person the Lord has called her to be. I thank God for bringing her into my life. She knows the Lord, and she has the courage and strength that can only come from knowing Him. She is a light to those who know her.

There I was at her wedding on a Caribbean island. I never thought I would see this day, but God is truly in the details. My mum attended this marriage. She had come a long way but she wanted to be there. Throughout the wedding, my mum would reflect on her life and be more open than she is normally. I challenged her by asking did she know Jesus as her Lord and Savior, did she believe that He died on the cross for us and to forgive all our sins (past, present, and future). Did she believe that He was resurrected on the third day and that He is still alive? Had she repented of her sins? She said yes. I assured her that is a good thing and she will go to heaven. My mum was so caring; she did not have much materially but she would give you her last penny if you needed it. The story of the widow's mite always reminds me of her.

September 9, 2012: I am in church on my own. I remember I was back in that place at work; again, on a project that I found challenging with a difficult client. I was asking the Lord to change things for me and to take me away from the project. I sat down after praise and worship, ready to hear what the Lord wanted to say to me through the pastor. I received a text. "Mum's died, call home."

What? Can this be true? I had only seen her at the wedding two months ago, and left her at the airport planning her next trip to come see me. "Mum's died, call home." How those words have stuck with me. I didn't know what to do. My husband had soccer commitments that morning, which meant he could not come to church. I stood up and walked out.

People I knew were saying hello and giving me high-fives as I left. All I could think was, "Oh my, how could this have happened?"

I walked out of the sanctuary and that is when I saw a pastor who asked me what was the matter. I held my phone up to him and show him the message. He takes me into a room. I break down and scream from the bottom of my heart. How cruel. I did not get a chance to say goodbye, but I really had. I had the assurance that she is in heaven, but it certainly did not feel that way as I sat in the room and poured my heart out.

A friend came by to comfort me, one I had been thinking of that very morning and thought I had not seen for a long time. Now here she was at my side, comforting me. Oh, how God is in the details.

My husband comes to me and we hurried to make flight arrangements, and were fortunate enough to get a flight out that day. "Mum has died. Call home." How those words resonated all the way home to England.

Upon arrival, I was greeted by my siblings. My youngest sister was the most devastated, as she was with Mum every day. They were inseparable. I can't say I was Christ-like on the trip. There were several moments that challenged me. When I should have taken a deep breath and called on the Lord for wisdom and strength, I relied on my own flesh, which is never good. After five days, I left to fly back to the United States, tormenting myself with thoughts that I had not been the Christian I had been called to be. I have repented and know my Lord has forgiven me. I will not let that stick with me.

My mum had apparently gone to bed that night and had a heart attack and died in her sleep. In hindsight, a good way to go, with no pain or suffering; not a good place for those left behind. It is a reminder for me that we are not guaranteed our next breath and we should live each day as though it's our last; expressing our love to all, even our enemies. I know it's hard, isn't it, because life happens and we don't always live that way. Imagine what a difference the world would be if we all lived as though today would be our last.

Prior to my mum's sudden death, I was again not in a good place with work. I was reminded of my colleagues' advice that the firm is all about its people and if you are a good performer, they will help you find the right role for you. I had seen a position I thought was perfect for me. It sounded and looked like a job that I had done several years ago. All the people with whom I sought for advice told me that I should not take it, as it was a step back. I was on track for the next level role, so I would be taking a giant step of faith.

Then my mum dies. It was during my time away from work, which was less than two weeks, that I reflected on my life and how our lives on this earth are really temporary and we are mortal. How many times I've asked the Lord to come back soon to take me away so I can live with Him forever and ever. Then I look about and see my unsaved family and friends, and think maybe not just yet.

So here I am again, thinking what's next. I thought I'd heard from the Lord that I should go for the position which, in human terms, seems like a step back. I have three reasons, which I shared with others why I should go for this role.

First, it gives me an opportunity to broaden my knowledge about the firm; second, it gives me an opportunity to increase my network, because remember it's all about people and relationships; and third, it was about the opportunity to have an impact on people's lives.

I could use this as an opportunity to be a light. I would meet more than a thousand people in the next two years in this role. I related it to being like a pebble in the pond. In client service roles, I dealt with one to two clients a year on their organizations. In this role, I would meet over a thousand consultants. That is a minimum: a thousand clients, a thousand families, a thousand communities. How much more of an impact is that? Such a no-brainer. It's an opportunity to really use the talents and skills I've been given. Another reasons I shared with some people was that I had the role tell me this was a gift from Him. How could I turn down a gift from the Lord?

I contacted the hiring manager, and he was ready to hire me immediately. However, I was in a client-facing role and we had to negotiate with the client. My project manager was not happy that I had chosen the other role, as I had built a great relationship with the client. For the first time, this client saw the value of the focus on people and not just on the bottom line.

December 2012: I started my new role and loved it. I'm meeting so many people. Getting the opportunity to share my story with them and being able to put myself in their shoes. I'm training new, experienced hires that have joined the firm; people just like me. Except now they are being trained on what it's like to join the firm, with training that I never received. I am able to share how they may be feeling about joining one of the world's largest consulting firms. They may be feeling inadequate, that they are not good enough; they may be feeling insecure; they may need to go and Google words that some people use because it's a very different language. Then I'm able to give them hope that if they persevere, this feeling too will pass. I am living proof of standing in front of them, because I survived. Many people would come to me at the end of the training and share how my stories touched them, and they could totally relate. I would thank Jesus for putting me in the role. Several times, He would remind me of this gift.

Over time, this role changed. Well, actually, the role did not change; I changed. Here I was traveling every other week to a big city in America to educate a fresh group of experienced new hires. I had gained experience of conducting different types of training, blending learning programs that involved face-to-face training, use of online learning meetings, and online collaboration tools. I was meeting so many people, including external consultants, and comparing myself to them. Look here I go again, comparing myself to my colleagues. This time I was probably the most experienced of the team, because of my previous backgrounds. It was a safe place to be where I could shine. Plus, I can use this experience to be a coach to others.

Why did I change? I started to get bored. The role was not challenging anymore. Why did I feel like I needed to put myself in a place that was challenging? In a role where I would wake up feeling sick each morning? Didn't the Lord say this is a gift that I am using the talents that I have been given? So why did I feel bored? Have you ever been in that place where you are actually being used to your full potential, you are impacting others' lives, and yet, you feel bored? You are looking for something more. Why does the flesh do that? I'm reminded of Adam and Eve. I believe they were not satisfied in the garden; they had to go and taste the fruit, and so the fallen world was created. That's why we live in a fallen world, and because we are human, there are times when we feel dissatisfied and seek some of the fruit.

I put myself in a place where I started doubting the gift. What am I doing here? It's time to go back into client service to the world that whilst I was a top performer did not fully satisfy me! We also figured as a family it was time to move to another state. So, I started to play God. I began to play with the chess pieces of my life. I figured if I do this and that, then this would cause X and Y to happen. Ever heard the phrase, "Man makes plans and God laughs"?

I was trying to figure out how to make my plan work. I didn't see the whole picture and I certainly didn't go to the Lord very often. I kept going back and forth, thinking, *Should I stay in this role until the end of my assignment; should we move to another state?* Sometimes I heard a faint reminder of the gift. My team members would remind me of what it is like compared to being in this role, versus a client-facing role. I would even speak to people who were planning to apply for my role and sell the benefits of the role that I was planning to leave. Could I hear myself speak?

I decided I was going to leave the role a few months before it was up so I could follow the development cycle, which impacts performance appraisals because it's all about performance, right?

I have a couple more training sessions to complete. I want to perform as many as I can, so that I can get to meet many people. My daughter is home and I have to travel out-of-state again. I work it with a colleague that I only need to be in the session for two days and not four. I probably could have had him cover the full four days, but no, I wanted to be leaving on a good note and be a strong performer. I fly out of state to lead the session.

2014

February 2014: One of the worst storms hits the East Coast. I am working in Chicago. Have I not seen any of the news predicting this. Of course not, because I don't watch TV. What a time-waster!! I go to the session with the plan to leave in the late afternoon of day two. The snow begins to fall in midafternoon. I received a text that my flight is canceled and I will not be able to get out until Thursday. Okay, so I'm meant to be here the full four days; is that what this is all about? But what about time with my daughter at home, is that not also important?

The snow is coming in really hard in my hometown that very rarely gets snow. I text my daughter on day three's morning, telling her that I wish I was at home and not sure why I'm here stuck in the city. She reminds me that everything happens for a reason, so let's try not to worry. When we worry, we take our eyes off God as we worry because things appear to be out of our control. Except what we forget is that nothing is really in our control, other than the decisions we make around free will.

Day three, still no good signs of getting home. I'm in a meeting with a colleague and my phone rings. It's my daughter. I tell the colleague I will get it later and she encourages me to answer. My daughter is crying hysterically on the phone. "Mum" she is screaming, "Mum, Mum, Snowy has been hit by a car!"

Oh no! My precious dog. I had tried to convince my husband to get a pet and finally, after twenty-five years, we get one. The dog was given to me as a surprise birthday gift. He was just a six-week-old pup. He was a bundle of white fluff. My husband and daughter had bought him for me because I was spending more time working from home and they wanted me to have some company while they were gone. Now my precious dog, who is five years old, has been hit by a car! I hear my daughter crying on the phone. My husband comes on the phone to relate the story of what happened.

They had both gone out in the snow to find a place to sledge. The dog was not on his leash, as there was too much snow on the ground for any traffic. Plus, we live out in the boonies, in the middle of nowhere. Still, my daughter carried the dog when she got to the road and the place to sledge. My husband had told her she could put him down. At that time, a car appeared from out of nowhere and the dog ran at the car.

Only the week previous I was walking my dog in the park and thinking that I should take him to training to stop him from running at cars! Was it my fault that I had not done the training sooner?

The car hit him but did not stop. Why would it? It probably did not see him and it felt like it had gone over a bump in the snow. My dog was only eleven pounds. My daughter tells me how my dog sat up on his front paws, looked at them with a shocked look on his face, almost like he was saying, "What just happened?"

They picked him up and ran to the car. The driveway was covered with snow, too steep to get the car out. As my husband relays the story, I hear them trudging in the snow as they walked to the nearest animal hospital, which is almost a mile away. Walking in the streets can be treacherous, especially as there are no sidewalks, plus with the deep snow makes it not ideal. I hear my daughter trying to comfort my dog. I am hysterical in the office, praying, "Dear Lord, please don't take my dog away." It was only the previous week we were snuggling him and telling him how much we loved him, and what joy he had brought to our lives.

A colleague tries to reassure me he has probably gotten a broken leg and will be okay. I reminded her of the time my sixteen-year-old best friend was hit by a car and I went to bed, thinking I would see her the next day in the hospital and she would have a broken leg. No, my friend was killed instantly! I could see this happening to my dog, except he is now in pain.

Ten minutes later, I received a call from my husband. They could not save my dog. I'm devastated and break down in tears. I take my glasses off and throw them on the table. No one can console me. My boss tries to calm me by showing that maybe the reason I was here is that I did not have to experience that. How could he say that? If I was at home, this would not have happened. Doesn't he know that? Don't I know that everything happens for a reason and God is in the details? When your time is up, your time is up. Your date and time are in the Book of Life. Whatever you do can't change that. It was my dog's time, even though that was hard to accept.

Now I have to try and find a flight out! Crazy, all flights are booked. I have to console myself and come to the realization that I'm not going to get home anytime soon. My colleagues take me back to the hotel and give me a drink to console me, but that only makes me worse. How does drinking glasses of alcohol console one, especially when it's gin, which is supposed to make you sad?

I become quite loud in the bar area and I challenge the server as to whether she believes in Jesus and if not, she should so that she knows where she is going when she dies! I don't think at that moment in time I am being a good representative of Christ. How can someone who clearly has had too much to drink be trying to convert people? I finally am taken up to my room. I readily get on the phone and start calling my dear friends, sharing the news of my dog with them. I'm truly devastated and in shock!

Sometimes I think I was sadder about my dog than about my mum. The only reason being that my dog was close to me each day whereas my mum was not. She was "across the pond," as they say in the States, plus we did not speak each week. Mum was always quite difficult to speak with, as she did not share her feelings but said everything was always fine.

Why did she try to protect me from what was happening back at home? Later, I learned from someone that fine stands for Feelings Inside Never Expressed or exposed. How true is that? Next time you hear someone say they are fine, challenge them and asked them how they really feel. You may be surprised at the response.

Back to my dog: I am able to connect with a few close friends. Of course, they feel sorry for me. I go to bed in a drunken stupor, after I had previously thrown up in the bathroom. I wake up the following day in a fog. I am stuck in this huge city with nowhere to go because of the snow. Crazy, I just had an aha moment stuck in snow and my Snowy is killed!

Of course, I can go and try make the course and lead it. The show must go on. Plus, I am an extrovert. I will go crazy if I was to stay cooped up in this hotel room all day, waiting to hear if I can get out in this weather. I head to the office and arrive at 7:30 am. The class is due to start at 8 am. I convinced my team I'm good to go. This will be good for me; and it was. Also, I thought I was able to focus on what I was doing, on the learners and doing a great job! In the breaks, I am desperately connecting with my admin team to see if I could get out.

The airline said they had a flight for later that afternoon. How could that be? The airport was supposed to be closed down. Oh well, Lord, if you want me to go home early, I know You of all people can make it happen. I tell my learners I am leaving the session early and will be leaving them in very capable hands. I head over to the airport.

Have you ever been to an airport when flights are being canceled left, right, and center, and because of the weather? It is bedlam, chaos! People everywhere. There is a very long line. I patiently get in line and everyone around me is sharing the stories about the travel woes: luggage going missing, missing connecting flights, blah blah blah. All I know is my flight still shows that it is leaving today and I want to get home to my husband and daughter. I get closer and closer to the desk and the text arrives. Flight canceled! Oh no! Take a deep breath. It's out of my control and wait until I get to the desk to find out what the actual situation is.

I need to talk to a gate agent. Who knows how long he has been working, and how much hassle he has been getting? My motto is to kill people with kindness. You get more out of the bee if you give them honey than if you feed them vinegar. One of my one-liners, and I have many that I have gathered over the years. (See the end of this book for several of my one-liners.) I try to "butter him up" and share my story, but to no avail. I am on standby, and he reminds me that many people have been trying to get out for many days! Thankfully though I have status, thank you Jesus, and this time for all the travel I have been doing, I'm near the top of the standby list.

I get to the gate and see if I can butter up the next gate agent. While waiting in line, the agent makes an announcement if you are on standby, you are on the list. No need to wait in line, so I will sit and wait. I know that one of my team members comes in the office early so I am communicating to try and get on a different flight, a different airline maybe? Here I go trying to control! I decided to sit on the floor and read my Bible and wait.

Announcement made: there are sixty-seven people on the standby list and the flight is already full. Oh Lord, I need a miracle. Sit and wait, and make small talk to some people close to me. Apparently, there are a lot of people trying to get to Charlotte for a conference that starts today and goes through the weekend. I sit and read and wait.

Another announcement: the plane that is taking us to Charlotte has a mechanical issue and is delayed. Oh boy! People start moving about. I did not realize it is the very people who are trying to get to the conference that are now trying to fly on alternative planes; this begins to free up seats. Six people are called. Number seven, interesting number, Sephton. A wave of relief washes over me. I go to the counter and the lady asked me window or aisle. I really don't care; I just want a seat to get home. Ticket in hand, I think I got a window seat, my preference, and managed to go home, thank you Jesus. I can't remember the flight at all, as I slept all the way.

My daughter greets me and is very sad. We give each other a big hug. My husband comes up (no dog in the car). Kevin would always meet me with my dog when he picked me up, and my dog will be looking out the window with his big tongue hanging out. It was surreal; we try to make small talk as we drive home. It's funny how at times like this we don't want to talk about what happened and we put on brave faces.

We arrive home. Kevin and Angela had cleared out everything that belonged to the dog. We all have a group hug and cried. I collapsed to the floor on the rug, where I would normally play and tickle my dog. I just could not believe it. We decided to go and pick my dog up, aka get him from the hospital so we could bury him! I did not want to see him. I don't want to see people in their dead state but want to remember them when they were alive.

I recall when my friend Angela was killed at the age of sixteen and I went to visit her at home, yes at home. In those days, and especially in the Catholic religion, you would host the body in the house for number of days so that people could come and pay their respects. I went to Angela's house and sat down. I did not want to see my best friend in the coffin. Someone encouraged me to see her, but I said no. Not sure who it was, but they physically encouraged me to see her by dragging me over. I will never forget that!

I did not want to see my dog, but then when we got to the waiting room, I decided I did. Why do people say when they are talking about dead people how they look beautiful and peaceful? I know we are talking about a dog here but the same applies. I was okay they look so peaceful, or some other similar comment! Now I know that is simply the physical body that was in the coffin and the spirit is either in heaven or hell, depending on whether they accepted Christ as their Lord and Savior while they were alive or not.

I decide to see my dog. The box is brought in and Kevin lifts the lid, stiff as a board and cold, as if he had been in the freezer! No, put him back in the box. I sat my dog in my lap and take him home. Interesting that I am the one that handles the dead. I was the one that picked up my dad's ashes, as we went to bury him. I recall being amazed that a person could be turned into ashes and fit in the small space. I recall asking the man, "Is that my dad?" He simply nods. Of course, we know this is to be true; however, it still hurts and doesn't seem real. I was the one that went to pick up my mum's ashes and bring them home, so that as a family we could go and bury them with my dad. It still amazes me. Of course, depending on the circumstances, there is a time and place for you to take the lead. However, this is not healthy if this is the norm in your relationship.

So that was how I ended that last role, that was the gift. Here I am now waiting to go back into client service. I do some small projects and everything seems "fine." I am put onto a project with somebody that I had met when I was in my training role. It seemed like a good fit. Things seem to be going well, and then the thoughts start again. Once again, I'm back to thinking, "I can't do this." "I'm not good enough." "Why am I here?" I feel like I'm not connected with the team, and I now know that my actions probably will not be very welcoming because I know my thoughts would be creating my feelings, which then creates my actions. If I am thinking I'm not good enough, then I will act in a way that proves that I'm not good enough.

I keep telling my leader that I'm having issues, but remember he knew me from when he came to training. He knows how good I really am and encourages me to continue. I find myself in the hotel room. I am not being sick in the toilet this time; instead, I am walking around, pulling my hair out and saying to myself and out loud, "I can't do this, I can't do this, I can't do this." I get the flight home and my husband picks me up at the airport. He has the radio blaring with the song, "Happy." You know the one with the words about being happy with lots of handclapping. I asked him to turn the radio off; that I'm not feeling happy and I want to quit my job.

PART 2 – The Craziness Begins

All these triggers, large and small, led up to May 2014, when the craziness begins.

What follows next are the details of my crazy summer.

Hold on for the ride.

May 2014

My husband takes me home from the airport and tries to console me. I keep saying that I want to quit my job. I say that I will simply send an email to my partner and coach, just letting them know that I have quit. My husband does a great job of bringing me off the edge of the cliff and encouraging me to sleep and to wait until the morning when I'm refreshed.

I don't sleep, but toss and turn. At six am the next day, I make the call that in hindsight I can't believe I made. I call my partner and tell him that this is the hardest call I have had to make in all my career. I tell him that I want to quit my job. I'm crying and telling him that I can't do my job. I'm not good enough and don't know what to do.

At first, I don't think he took me seriously. No, it's six am, I AM serious. I really appreciate the fact that he spent two hours on the phone with me and we had lots of great conversations. He reminds me that I am not acting like myself, and that I need help. After much persuasion, I did not quit my job. Thank God! He tells me to take some time off and to get whatever help I need, and then I could come back to work. He said take five to seven weeks off and we should be good by them.

This is a Friday and I am meant to go to the client site on Monday. What am I going to do? Who is going to tell the leader of the project? He tells me that all would be taken care of and not to worry. He continues to remind me that this isn't like me, and that I am acting out of character. All I could say is, "I just can't do this anymore; I just can't do this anymore."

I call my best friend, my prayer partner Christine, and tell her what I have done, asking her to come and sit with me and pray with me.

While waiting for Christine to arrive, my old colleague Paul calls me. He shares a story about me wanting to either quit or take time off sick, and he compares that to me sitting in a dark cave and there's a door open. The door is actually cracked open and there is light on the other side, and all I have to do is to open the door and step out into the light from the dark and all will be good. He coaches me to think about the implications of me taking time off, especially that I am leaving the project midway. I tell him that I will pray about it and get back with him.

Now normally after this kind of conversation, I would change my mind and would continue to move on. However, this time is different and, in my mind, I am convinced I just couldn't do it; I am not able to just take that small step and open the door into the light. I call him back and share my decision. He is understanding, and says that this is very unusual for me.

Isn't it funny how the people that I spoke with on that day all mention the fact that my behavior is very unusual and not something that they are familiar with? So that's it; I have made the decision and I have decided to take a short period of time off work for a break.

My friend Christine arrives. She is really a good friend and prayer partner. I see my small devotional on the side table and pick up and go to the verse of the day. I can't remember exactly what it said; however, I do know that it clearly resonated with me and I knock myself for not being as committed to reading my daily devotionals.

In hindsight, I know that this is okay and that there is no rule that says I should read my devotional every day. Thank you, Jesus, for the gift of grace. I curl up like a little baby and feel quite lost. Christine leaves and my husband arrives. The next few days, I am bored and basically not doing very much. It's weird when Monday arrives, as this is when I am supposed to be at the client site in Memphis but I wake up and have nowhere to go and nothing to do. I call my doctor and make an appointment.

Now I am actually not a television watcher and all I could think to do is sit on the sofa. I had downloaded a few books because I thought now is a good time to read. The books that I read have titles like, "It's time to walk on the water." They are all books about stepping out in faith. It seems weird that I am reading those books, as if I am searching for something.

I get to see my doctor and she tries to put me on medication. I don't know what she thinks; she knows that I do not like to take medication. So, after a lengthy discussion, she agrees that I should take some time to rest and relax before I go back to work. As the days go by, I continued to talk with my human resource contact, and they have to make a decision as to the length of time that I will be absent. I'm debating between using my vacation, taking time off sick, and other alternatives.

Throughout this time, my friend Christine comes to visit and we go out for walks. My husband continues to be a rock, and he ensures daily that I am exercising and eating.

I decide that I still need more time, but this means, however, that I may have to sign off on short-term disability. I'm thinking to myself I don't want to be classified as disabled, all because of the word disability in short-term disability. How crazy was I to think like that! So, after some long debates with my husband and my friend, I agree to continue my time off. This means that I have to go back to the doctors to get verification of my sick time.

This time with my doctor, she asks me to take medication and convinces me that it will help. She also encourages me to go seek a counselor or therapist. As part of my medical benefits at work, I am entitled to go and see a counselor for free. So why not take the advantage? I clearly need to do some work at this level.

The Counsellors

Counsellor #1: Here I am sitting in my "free" counselling session. I have the mindset that nothing is really free – even Christ paid a price for my freedom.

Let's see how this lady can help me. I can be so critical and judgmental at this time. I need to speak to someone who really knows me and God. I do my "intake" and through all this, all I seem to be doing is "judging" the person. In my role as a facilitator and coach, I am very comfortable with feedback mode. Of course, I don't verbally give feedback to this person, but oh boy it is all going through my mind.

"Well, that was not the right question to ask!"

"That was a leading or multiple question – how do you expect me to answer?"

"I know where you are going with this line of questioning!"

"I figured it all out – why am I here?"

One of the things that she asks me to do, which on reflection was a good "exercise." I was asked to go home and find a shoebox, decorate it, and put all my negative thoughts in there, then close it and it's done! Simple, right?

This lady is near Christine's house. She helps me to find a shoebox. I go home and go through the motions. I decide I can't really decorate it – not sure what to use. Instead of using wrapping paper, I decide to take post-its and on each one, I put my favourite Bible verses so that

I am constantly reminded of these as I put in my negative thoughts: "Why am I here? What's this all about? I'm not needed! God has left me!" Once I decorated it and put in my thoughts, that's it – used it once and left it alone. In hindsight, there is something about putting thoughts in a box. However, if you don't deal with them, then something is going to knock the lid off and those thoughts come flying out to be dealt with!

I continued to go see this lady for five sessions. That is what I was entitled to: five free sessions. I'm sure she helps me; at the time, I am thinking I could do her job!

Counsellors #2 and #3: My friends Christine and Diana.

They would spend time with me, listen, and question. I know both have my best interest at heart. As both are Grace Life International Counsellors, they are helping me by confirming my faith and my relationship with Christ. I know that Christine isn't too sure about taking medication. I believe Diana is. Diana is quite prophetic, and I recall her saying something like, "If you don't get help, you will end up in a psychiatric ward, and that is not where you want to be." How did she know I would end up there? Thankfully for only a short period, but it was long enough to know that is not an experience I would choose to repeat.

When I am in "the resort," (the resort is my fun name for the psych unit) Diana gives my husband counsel to share with me. "Tell Elaine not to talk about God; they won't understand; and they will just think she is crazy." This is one of the first conversations I had with my doctor:

Doctor: "Do you see anything? Have hallucinations?"

Me: "No."

Doctor: "Do you hear voices?"

Me: "Yes, but I know it's Satan, and I tell him to leave me alone !"

Doctor must think: "Yup, we have a crazy one here."

I think: "I have conversations with God and Satan all the time. Isn't that what Christians do?"

You guessed it! They thought I was crazy.

Counsellor #4: Is she really qualified? After much resistance, I agree to my doctor's advice and I make an appointment with a Christian counsellor. She is not connected with my church or with Grace Life International. How did I find her – God, of course, leads me to her. However, He uses a friend to tell me about the counselling through a local church. I look at the website and find the page with counsellors. How do you decide?? I started going through their bios and based on this, I make my choice. My counsellor has a PhD; however, she didn't have the counselling initials after her name. The first session with her, I question her credibility – why don't you have the same qualifications as everyone else? Well, I know now, a PhD is far more superior, duh! What this means to me is that I am getting the most qualified person in this group. In hindsight – thank you Jesus.

My sessions with her are quite volatile. One minute I am crying; the next minute I am shouting, I don't recall ever laughing. I was shouting at her and questioning was she a believer. I told her I needed more faith. She would respond with you needed to go see a psychiatrist. I tell her I'm not going to because all they would do is give me drugs, and that is not what I need.

Her rationale to see a psychiatrist goes like this. I have a broken head that needs help! She explains that for most people, if they have issues with their bodies, from the neck down, they go see a doctor. When there are issues from the neck upwards, that is a taboo and people don't want to deal with this. I get the logic but still didn't want to go. I would scream and shout – at least I didn't get physical.

My primary care doctor is still in touch with me. I give permission for my psychiatrist and doctor to speak to each other. I'm sure they have lots of notes to compare. Between them, they are telling me to go see a psychiatrist. After about four sessions, I'm not sure what causes me to change my mind but I decide to say yes.

Not sure if you have ever tried to make an appointment with a psychiatrist – not that easy! It's amazing how many of them are fully booked and as a new patient, you can't get in to see them for many weeks. What if I was really ill? What would I have done – suppose go to the ER!

I am able to make an appointment in approximately one week's time for a psychiatrist who is pretty local. Why is he open? Why is he not fully booked? Is he a bad doctor? Why is my mind working overtime? I should be grateful that I got to see someone so quickly. I hope he is a Christian.

More about this experience in the next chapter. I want to conclude this chapter with my other counsellors. The friends who thought they were being helpful, but really all they did was add to the confusion.

Kevin is out of town and I drag myself out of bed to go to church. I didn't want to be seen in the section I would normally sit. I want to hide and sit in the complete opposite section. Hopefully none of my friends see me.

The service ends and I see a friendly face. I go over to see her and break down crying. Why did I, first of all, want to be in a section that I was "hiding" and then reach out to a friend? I know my poor friend didn't know how to respond to me. She did what she could. However, there are a couple of church elders close by – friends of mine. They start praying for me and anoint me with oil.

I recall the guy telling me that I belong to Jesus and it will be OK. He even comments on the fact that I have a cross design on my dress. He likens this to Jesus being all around me. He has to leave to run an errand, so his wife and my friend take a trip to Panera Bread; a place where a lot of people go to after church. Please let us just get our food and hide in a corner booth.

We situate ourselves, but I don't eat. By this time, I may have lost twenty-five pounds in weight. I'm not eating well, and all the nervous energy means that whatever I am eating simply burns off really fast.

Here we are sitting in the booth. The older lady is sitting across the table from me, with my friend to her side. She opens the Bible and starts to recite Scripture. She tells me all I need is more faith, which to me feels like I am losing God and He isn't there for me. What could I do to get more faith? She tells me that I didn't need drugs; I simply need to pray more, and that I didn't need to go and see a psychiatrist. She has no medical grounds upon which to make these statements. Believe it or not, she does take pills for her high blood pressure! In hindsight, guess the psychologist is right. People will find it ok to get treatment and see a doctor for anything that is not related to the brain – or, in her words, from the neck up. Why couldn't my friend simply pray away her high blood pressure? She didn't have enough faith!

Now I am convinced that I am losing God and it's all about my faith!

Another friend passes by the table. She looks at me and gives me a hug. She has no idea what our conversation has been about. When I get home, she calls me and says simply: "I want you to know I am praying for you. You don't need to tell me what's going on. I'm praying." That is so sweet. I couldn't have told her anyway – the shame! Later, she shares that she knew I was in a bad place by the way I looked.

I leave Panera Bread in a mess! What am I to do? Where am I to go? I have made my appointment with the psychiatrist, but I can cancel it. I know I will call and check if he is Christian. If he isn't, then I will cancel!

The Psychiatrist – Feeling Like Judas

It's the Friday before my seven-thirty am Monday morning appointment with the psychiatrist. I call his office and pose the question to His receptionist. "Is the doctor a Christian?" She doesn't know and will call me back.

A few hours later, she returns my call. The response: "He doesn't think that is relevant to the appointment." What? OF course, it is relevant to me. I only want to deal with Christians; no one else will understand me. Looking back, she didn't give me an option to cancel. She simply said, "Look forward to meeting you on Monday."

It's only Friday and I have to get through this weekend. I wait until eleven pm on the Sunday evening to complete the intake paperwork. I'm tired and clearly not in my best place. Looking at the questions, they didn't make sense. Why do I want to be at the meeting? Because I am a people-pleaser and I need to be a God-pleaser!

That evening I didn't sleep, like most evenings actually. This night, I have a crazy dream that I am in a fight with Satan and God. I think God is pulling me away and pulling me away from getting help. This must be a sign. I must not go see the psychiatrist.

We wake up early and I tell Kevin about my dream, and that we should not go to the appointment. He is having none of it. He dresses me and we are on our way. I feel so nervous and truly don't want to go. Oh, the thoughts that are going through my mind! As we walk across the parking lot to the doctor's office, I am thinking: "Oh my how inflation has gone. Judas betrayed Jesus for thirty pieces of silver. Here I was doing the same for $300." Yes, I feel like Judas, and yes, the visit is not covered by insurance, so I have to pay cash. What a rip-off and what a waste of money, I think.

So, I have struggled to go across the parking lot. I really feel forced into this appointment and really didn't want to be there. It was 7:30 am and I am the first one there. The office is very intimate, almost like a home. The lady in the front desk asks me a few questions and then I have to wait. The waiting period is not very long. My husband stays in the waiting room as the doctor calls me in. I did not want to have my husband in the room with me. Not sure why; I just did.

I see a sofa in the doctor's room. I smile, as it reminds me of all the TV programs that I have seen that involve a visit to a psychiatrist office. I stay clear of the sofa and head to the chair. I'm sure that there is some psychology behind the reason why I did that; I wonder if the doctor makes a note.

Here I am in the office of a psychiatrist – I really can't believe it.

His first question: "What brought you here today?"

Me: "I don't know, because I'm a people-pleaser and not a God-pleaser."

I also challenge him by saying: "You are not really interested in listening to me; you are just going to prescribe me drugs." He nods his head and said "Yes." My psychologist is my therapist; my psychiatrist is my drug doctor!!

I really can't recall much of the remainder of the conversation. All I remember is having a discussion on the topic of medication and he is giving me choices. How am I supposed to make a choice in the state of mind I am in? I couldn't even choose to get out of bed in the morning without my husband helping me (or should I say forcing me, because that is the only way I got out).

He tells me all the options of the different kinds of medication. I sit there and ponder – I really didn't know. He ends up saying to me, "Well you don't have to make a decision now; you can call me later. However, you can't sit here all day; I do have other appointments."

In that moment, I agree to take a prescription. Then off I go home and get the prescription filled. Who knows what the medication is called?

All I know is that I look up the medication on the internet and it has ridiculous side effects – why is death a side effect??? Plus, it states that it is an addictive drug! I didn't want to become an addict, so I decide not to take the medication. I put it to one side.

The week is as traumatic as normal; it has become my new normal. Get up with my husband in the morning and go for a walk. Off he goes to work – of course he had to; there is nothing he could do while I'm feeling sorry for myself! I sit alone and listen to the clock at the top of the hour. It used to chime; however, I turned it off, and all I heard in the silence is the clicks as it hits the hours. Why did time continue to move on? Oh, how I wish it would stop!

In the afternoon, I would go sit with my elderly neighbor. (I know she would not like me calling her elderly, even though she was in her 70s! She was pretty great for her age.) Her life had been very traumatic. She had lost both her daughters to cancer, lost her husband early, and had one surviving son who thankfully lived nearby. So, she would encourage me by telling me to "pull up my boot straps" and just get going. I would tell her I'm waiting for Jesus, and she would respond with: "God helps those who help themselves." I know that is flawed thinking. It's amazing how many people would offer advice like: "You just have to get over it," and "This too will pass."

I honestly can't recall what the evenings looked like when my husband got home. I likely sat in a daze as he ate dinner and watched TV. Thankfully it is the summer time, which meant that he didn't have soccer practice in the evenings.

The week passes and I go to my follow-up psychiatrist appointment on Monday.

The doctor asks how the medication worked for me. I tell him I didn't take it, as I didn't want to be addicted. So, he says OK and prescribes me another medication. He also asks how I'm sleeping. Not very well, I tell him. I spend most of the night awake. I have moved out of the bedroom with my husband, because I want to be in complete darkness alone. He also prescribes a sleeping medication.

I go home with my husband and fill both prescriptions. Go home and check the internet. I'm not taking the medication for my head. I don't like the side effects; however, I will try the sleeping medication. I put the medication to one side. I'm getting quite a stash now!

The sleeping medication is not helpful. I have the most vivid dreams, not nightmares, but dreams that are so real, and yet so unreal. I recall a lot of space travel dreams. Have you ever had dreams that you wish you wrote the dream down when you woke up, because you are certain they could make a movie of it? Oh, I wish I had written down those dreams.

In the days that passed, I would continue to journal a lot. I would go to the park and simply sit and write. I recall having a whole dialogue with myself: Jesus or drugs?? I was so conflicted still. Maybe I will give the drugs one more chance? In the park one day, I call my psychiatrist. He is very accessible which I appreciate. I go back to my conversation with him about my conflict regarding drugs. He says to me something that I am very familiar with:

"What's the definition of insanity? Doing the same thing over and over again, expecting different results!"

I knew that. You have probably heard it, but we or should we say *I* don't want to do anything different. Different is challenging and I don't want a challenge; I'm scared to change.

The week passes and back I go for my third appointment. I report that the sleeping medication doesn't work for me, so I had stopped taking them, and I have not started to take the other drugs.

Let's try one more time. I promise to take the medication this time. He gives me a prescription, and I go fill it. This time, I don't check the internet. I'm going to give it a try.

At this time also, my husband has planned to go to Brazil for the World Cup with his boys' soccer team. A once-in-a-lifetime-experience for them, but not for him. We have both been to South Africa for the 2010 World Cup with a different boys' team. The Brazil trip has been planned for a year and I encourage him to go. This would be the last time he would see the boys, as we are moving to Florida. Not sure if I have mentioned this part of the story yet…more to follow on that.

It's important we take a detour from the psychiatrist to talk about the ten days my husband had gone on the trip. This was during the time that I was going to the psychiatrist.

Don't think bad that my husband went to Brazil. I had encouraged him to go. I recall as he sat in the Charlotte airport how we were talking about moving to Florida or staying in North Carolina. Kevin had already given his notice to the club and told them he was leaving. His role had been divided between two people.

We sat in the airport and before he had to leave to go through security, we decided that we were staying and not leaving. I didn't feel well enough to make the transition. He called his former boss with the decision to stay. His boss told him he would always have a job with the club. Phew! We would be ok. Off he goes through security and onto Brazil.

July 2014 - He's Away, I will Play

So, my husband is away for ten days. Yay!! Well actually – oh no! What am I going to do? Friends have offered for me to stay with them. I do. First set of friends are local. I am able to stay at their lake house. They are a wonderful Christian couple and simply love on me and care for me. Lots of prayers are prayed.

I return to my own home – I can't stay with my friends all the time, even though they say I can! Home is very lonely! Listening to the clock ticking and hitting the top of the hour; sleeping in the darkest room and not feeling like I want to get out of bed. Still sleeping in a different bedroom because it is completely dark.

I'm taking medication now. I decide to go and visit a friend and her family in Atlanta. I can drive. It will do me good to get away for a few days. I make the call and arrangements are made.

I pack my bag the night before and I will get up early in the morning to make the few hours' drive. Oh my! I didn't sleep. In the morning, it takes all the strength that I have to get out of bed. I felt like Satan was trying to prevent me from going.

It is a real spiritual battle to get out of bed. I have to physically drag myself out and talk through each motion. One step into a leg of my pants, and then the next. Shirt on. Did I get washed?? I couldn't eat breakfast; I will eat when I arrive; I just needed to get out of the house.

I get on the road to Atlanta, it feels like the longest and toughest ride I had ever taken. My mind is all over the place. I am travelling in the slow lane all the way. I can only describe the feeling of what it must be like when driving under the influence. I am under the influence but not drunk. Did the drugs influence me – surely not? I cling tightly to the steering wheel. I tell myself that I couldn't stop on the way. If I stop, I am convinced that I would turn back and I simply couldn't do that. Tightly I hold on for dear life. I am battling all the way, but I know I can do this. It reminds me of the song, "Jesus Take the Wheel" by Carrie Underwood.

I arrive safe and am exhausted. It is so great to see my friend and her family. I love the fact that she has Christian music playing in the background all the time. She is going through her own issues. I didn't want to be a burden; however, she assures me many times that I am not. I love the way she calls me "friend."

Sitting in her living room, with my friend's girls in earshot, I find myself sharing my crazy summer so far with her. I end up crying and shouting. Oh, my what must the girls think of me! I used to be the one comforting their mum and now she is comforting me. The first day is a blur. It is a Saturday and I know that I hardly ate anything. I sleep in one of the girl's rooms. Well, I can't say I sleep; I rest, well not even that; I lay in the dark.

My mind is all over the place. Instead of giving Kevin the time to have a break in Brazil, I am sending him texts that I can only imagine concerned him. I'm telling him, yes, we should go to Florida, and then the next text, no we stay in Charlotte. I am comparing ourselves to the Israelites who wandered for forty years on a trip that should have taken eleven days. He is so far away, and I know it isn't the best trip that he had been on!

I wake in the morning and feel nauseous. It's Sunday and we are going to church. Normally – when I was "normal" – I would love to go to church. Not now, I feel condemned. We pass a billboard. It reads: "Are you going to heaven or hell?" In my mind I said: "Hell." Of course, I know that I am going to heaven.

Sitting in church, I feel such a stranger. Similar to when I had been reading my Bible and everything I read was negative – I am the thorn, and the rich young ruler – it is the same with the preacher. Everything he says is twisted negatively in my mind. I am physically present, clearly not mentally. My mind is all over the place. Have you ever felt you are walking in a haze?? Like an out-of-body experience?

We leave church and my friends are excited to show me the German village called Helen in Georgia. It's like a replica village. I'm sure it would have been a wonderful experience if I was in the present and able to focus instead of being in my head all the time. Why do these thoughts keep coming in? The little girls are so excited, but I couldn't settle. All I want to do is get out of there and go back to the house. Sitting in the bedroom is my safety.

The girls want ice cream and are so excited. Please let me just go home. I tell my friends I can't be there. We get the girls ice cream and come back home.

It feels so normal to be in the room and alone, with me and my mind! I am thinking about going back to my real home. I didn't want to do the drive and had planned to go home that Sunday evening in the dark. Probably wasn't a good idea, because I am tired and driving in the dark without stopping could have been dangerous. But it's all good. I can do this. As I get ready to leave, a huge storm comes in. The rain is beating down. I can still leave, can't I? My friends encourage me to stay. I mean what did I really have to go home to? An empty house; Kevin wouldn't be back for a few days. They told me I could stay until Kevin arrives home. But no, I want to go home now. The thunder rolls in, the rain is torrential. I decide to stay the night and leave the next day. Is this God keeping me safe?

I toss and turn, waiting for morning to come. It does, thankfully, and I can go home. This time I wake up with the thought that today is the last day of my life! I'm screaming in the bedroom. I can't go home; I'm going to be killed on the drive. I can't go home at all – ever! What a difference a night makes. Yesterday, I was all ready to leave.

I lay on the bed crying that I know today is the day I will die. I had visions of my going underneath one of those long trucks. This is probably because several years ago my daughter and I were driving home from Atlanta. At the time of writing, I have just recalled that I'm in Georgia close to Atlanta. The thought of my day of death was likely brought about by a trip home from Atlanta. Weird that it was the same place – Atlanta! Hmm, weird.

Several years ago, my daughter and I were on our drive home after being at a photo shoot, for her.

We had just gotten on the road and the traffic on the interstate was at a standstill. We were at the beginning of the line of traffic. We were still for almost five hours. Of course, we got out of the car and talked to many of the drivers. What we learned was there had obviously been an accident. A lady had driven under one of the long trucks. They had to cut her out. She had died instantly.

So, there you have it. I was going to die the same way. I was telling my friends:

"I know we don't know when we are going to die, only God knows. However, I was convinced that today is the day that I am going to die." Was I trying to "play God" again?

My friends move between trying to be tough with me and then simply laughing and trying to help me see how silly my words are. But no, here I am screaming on the bed,

"You don't understand, I'm telling you today I am going to die." I throw the pills on the bed and say that I need to stop taking them. My friend is a nurse and she tells me that I should not go cold turkey on the pills. My arms are beating the bed. Why am I here?? I can't go home.

My friends manage to calm me down. I take some deep breaths and decide to go home rather than stay a few more days. I do ask that they come with me to the gas station. My tire looks low and I want to make sure there is enough air in it. Plus, I need to get some gas.

What sticks in my mind is that when we turn up to the gas station, my friend removes the old banana skins out of my door bucket. I had not been keeping my car clean. I feel a little embarrassed that she did this. Never mind, at least that helped.

My tires are checked, I have gas in the car, and the sun is shining. The storm has passed; it's going to be a beautiful drive home. Off I set. I'm no longer convinced that today is the day I am going to die. I feel quite good.

The sun is shining, the interstate is clear, with hardly any trucks on the road. I feel in a good place. I start thinking about going back to work. I think I may be ready to go back. I can drive home from Atlanta. I am ready to go back. I feel brave. As I get closer to Charlotte, my mood begins to change. I start thinking negative thoughts again. I will stop at Christine's on my way home. I will stop and say "hi."

Christine opens her front door and welcomes me with open arms and a hug. I start crying and tell her about my crazy weekend; it was so bad. I had been sending Kevin so many texts. He must have been worried, confused, and so far, away and not being able to do anything. He probably felt helpless. Christine offers for me to stay the night.

"Thanks, but I have to get home." Why? I was going home to an empty house. But that is my house and my "safe place," which is so not true. In hindsight, it is the worst place for me to be. The isolation is not good. Staying in a dark bedroom most of the day is not good. However, I thought it was good as I didn't have to bother anyone. After staying a little time with Christine, I head home to my "nice" dark bedroom. Kevin would be home soon.

End of July 2014 - The Week Before

Kevin arrives home, and we are back to "normal." He makes sure that I get up in the morning and we go for a walk to get some exercise. We have breakfast, and he goes to work. I lay on the sofa and have many unhelpful conversations in my head. I'm trying to plan my next moves.

In the afternoons, I go to my neighbor's house and sit with her whilst she watches the TV and reminds me that I need to pull up my boot straps.

Sometimes I join Christine for walks around the mall. I also spend time with my friend Jennifer, who is going through her own issues. I'm there just listening. I have devoted a chapter to my friends.

Kevin is back from his Brazil trip. If you recall, he had quit his job, and then at the airport to Brazil he called his boss to tell him that we were not moving to Florida. His boss had said that he would still have work. Well what that meant was yes, he did still have work, but not his previous well-paid job. That had already been divided and given to two other people. (I always told him that he was doing a lot more than what he was being paid for.)

I am sitting at home in the "office." Kevin comes home after a meeting with his previous boss. He tells me that yes, they are able to take him back. Phew! But not at the same rate. He will be in a much-less paid role. Oh no, what are we are going to do? I'm not going to be able to work anymore; I'm going to lose my job (that's what I thought at the time) and my husband is not working in a well-paid job. How will we cope??? Without money, what will we do?

Kevin assures me it's all good and we will be OK. Hmm, I'm not so sure. My mind is churning all the time. One thought lead to another and soon, I'm spiraling down.

Instead of spending my days on the sofa in the living room, I choose to go down into the basement. Although it's a walk-in basement that has sliding doors and a window, it's still a lot less light; it's darker, and that suits me fine. I can sit in the dark place and ruminate on my thoughts when I am all alone.

I still go for my walks with Kevin each morning. It's Friday. We finish our walk with a visit to Starbucks. As I collect my drink, the barista asks me,

"What are your plans for today?"

Out loud, I reply, "Oh nothing much," and smile. In my head, I say, "I'm going to kill myself!"

Kevin had been on day one of an external 2-day course. I tell him laughingly what I had said to the barista and what I had said in my mind. He tells me that he is not going to finish the course and that he will stay at home with me.

Me: "Please don't stay at home. You need to go and do your course."

Kevin: "Uh no! I'm not letting you kill yourself!"

Me: "Don't be stupid, you don't really think I would do something like that. I will be ok."

Eventually, Kevin leaves and I go across to my neighbors. All is good. Of course, I am not going to kill myself.

Another week passes and I'm having conversations with my friend Christine; at times, I'm simply on my bed crying and will throw my phone down as I'm talking to her. I can't do this anymore.

I take my trips to the park and sit in my car and write in my journal. I have shared my journal at the end of this book. This will help those of you who have not been where I was (thankfully), and for those of who may have been, or who are currently going through this, to help give you reassurance that you are not crazy, and the experience is real. However, there is hope and if you have gotten this far in the book, you will, of course, realize that I didn't kill myself, and I am using my experience to give you hope for a brighter future.

The weekend arrives and it's a special weekend. Liverpool FC (the best football – or soccer team, as Americans would say – in the world), are playing in Charlotte. Of course, we have to go and see them play. Kevin loves that team; his whole family does.

As a side note, I was raised as a Blue (Everton) and not a Red (Liverpool). In Merseyside, in the "old days," Catholics supported Everton, and Protestants supported Liverpool. I know, crazy, right? Because I was raised Catholic, my dad told me I had to support Everton. Crazy, right? Religion creates so many "laws and rules" that cause so many problems. As a Christian, I am free to say that I support Liverpool as much as I support Everton. I'm not religious; I have a relationship with Jesus Christ, my Lord and Savior. I know for many of you reading this, that may sound crazy, and I understand, because I also thought the same before I was "saved" in 2001/2.

I digress, back to watching Liverpool FC in Charlotte. My husband's friend was in town and going to the game with us. We get ready to set off, and I stop and say I cannot go – this is the first time I will have been out in a crowd. A huge football stadium is really not my idea of my first trip out. No, I need to go to support my husband – he has a ticket for me; it will be a good game and a good experience. I stand there with my coat wrapped around me. I'm crying – should I stay or should I go? Sounds like I am back in Atlanta.

I gingerly walk down the steps of my house to the car. Kevin wants to leave, as he likes to be there before the start of the game and knows the traffic is going to be bad. He and his friend are sitting in the front of the car, and I get into the back. I leave the door open, as I am so indecisive. It really is crazy how now I can no longer make simple decisions. I am second-guessing everything. Ok let's do this. I close the door and off we go.

Quietly, I sit in the back, rocking back and forth to comfort myself. Have I made the right decision? Noooooo! I say in my head, I can't do this. We get closer to the stadium, and I see all the traffic and all the people. Everyone is so happy and excited to see the game. It's going to be great – I'm sure, but not for me.

I tell Kevin I can't do this and I have to go home. I know that he will know plenty of people at the game, so it will be no problem if I take the truck and drive back home. He can get a ride home.

"Really Elaine!" Kevin says.

"Yes, I can't do this, I can't go in. I have to go home," I say out loud. In my mind, I say, "I have to go back to my place of safety where I can be on my own."

Reluctantly, Kevin parks the truck, we swap seats, and I tell him to enjoy the game and off I go to drive home.

As I drive back, I start second-guessing again. I really should have stayed. I need to be there for Kevin. It's only a football game; it will be OK. What's going to happen to me? So, I pluck up enough courage and call Kevin.

"Hi love, I have decided I am going to turn around and come watch the game."

Kevin responds, "Sorry, we are in the stadium and I gave your ticket away to someone else."

It turned out that the person he gave it to was a big fan of Liverpool FC and they had lost their ticket, and so Kevin was able to give them mine. It was awesome they got to see the game, but not so good for me.

Guess I am meant to go home and stay in my happy place. I will go and spend some time with my neighbor.

Kevin and his friend come home. It was a great game and great atmosphere. I'm happy for them, but sad for me that I didn't get to experience it the way they did. All good, another time maybe. As a side note, I did return to Charlotte to watch Liverpool FC (2017).

August 2014 – the Day Arrives

Sunday, time to go to church. This used to be a joyful time for me, and now it's become a burden. Not sure why we keep going, as I believe at this stage that God no longer is with me, and He has left me – which I now believe is so untrue. He never leaves me nor forsakes me. (Deut. 31:8)

I recall in the service the pastor saying something along the line of "People pay $100s to go see a psychiatrist, when they can go to Jesus and it's free!"

I look at Kevin! And when we get out, I tell him:

"See I told you, I shouldn't be going to see the psychiatrist. I shouldn't be taking drugs. I need to trust in Jesus!"

Kevin replies, "Elaine, you are taking what the pastor said out of context. It's not for you."

Out of context – really, I have a clear mind (not!). Of course, I know he was talking to me.

I will break here to let you know that later I did have a conversation with the pastor about the impact of his story, and he shared that he is fully supportive of medication for the right reasons. Of course, not if you are taking illegal drugs or addicted to them. People take medication all the time, and based on my story, he would have been one of the first ones to take me to see a doctor.

Back to Sunday: Kevin and I continue to speak in the car going home, and I realize he is not going to understand me so I will be quiet.

Kevin takes off for soccer; it's good for him to get out. I feel sorry that he has to be in the house with me all the time.

As I sit in the house alone, I see all the medication that has been building up as I had been getting prescriptions filled and not taking them. Now I realize why this is. I have a cache of drugs that I can use to kill myself. I have this overwhelming desire to end it all. Before I have had the thoughts and said to myself such things as,

"Oh, while I'm driving if I could just crash into this tree, it would be ok." Or, "Oh it would be so easy to …"

But now on this Sunday, I am going to do it. I feel so lost and so hopeless. What is the reason for me living – I couldn't think of anything. I couldn't see myself getting better. I had already lost the Lord, so let's do this. I am home alone; I have the means and I can do it.

I grab hold of the pill bottles. I am wandering around my house crying. The tears are rolling down my face as I cry out to Jesus.

"Really, really Lord, is this what this has come to?"

"I can't believe it has come to this!"

"This is the only way out."

"Lord! Lord! Really!"

As I look back on this, I realize I was desperate to hear from Him. I was still crying out to Him. Somewhere deep down in my soul, I knew that I was not a child of Satan but a daughter of the Living God.

I'm crying and wandering. I've opened the pills and some of them drop on the floor. I'm scrambling to pick them up. I feel like an addict. I once heard in one of my Grace Life meetings when someone shared his story of being an addict how he had dropped pills on the floor and would scramble to pick them up. Each pill was so precious to him. Now here I am doing the same thing. I pick up the pills and wander and cry.

I know what I am going to do. I need to leave a note so that when Kevin finds me, he understands why I did this.

I'm curled up in the chair with my pills, writing my note, the tears are streaming down my eyes. I'm Googling, "Do Christians still go to heaven if they commit suicide?" Of course, some websites say yes and some say no. I will agree with the ones that say no because I have lost Jesus, right?

In my letter, I try to help Kevin understand this is nothing to do with him. I am telling him how to access my cell phone and giving him the passcode so that when he finds me, he can make all the calls, especially the call to work.

In the middle of writing the letter, my phone rings. It's my friend Julie. Julie had been calling me sometimes. She had moved out to California so she couldn't physically be here. Of course, I am not going to answer the phone. What do I say?

"Hi Julie, sorry I can't talk right now – I'm about to kill myself!"

Nope, I just let it ring; she will leave a voicemail and later learn why I didn't answer the phone.

That's it, letter's written. Next thing, where can I be found "dead"? What is the best position? What is the best place? The chair? The sofa? So many choices one has to make when deciding to end it all. As I look back now, it truly was God's way of having me "kill time," excuse the pun.

I found the chair and the position. I have the pills in my hand. One last cry out, "Lord, really, this must be it. I still can't believe what this has come to."

I cup my hands to my mouth and take some pills. I don't ingest them because my phone pings. It's a text from Kevin, he's on his way home! Now I can say looking back, "Thank you Lord for answering my cries. You were there still and You are with me now."

This is my wake-up call. I sit up. Pick up my pills. Put them back in the bottles. Take my letter and hide it. I'm ok. Nothing is wrong.

Kevin arrives home, and I act like "normal" in my eyes. He will tell you differently. We go to our neighbor's house and have dinner. In my mind, this is my last supper as I will kill myself tomorrow. I think I am being normal at dinner, apparently not according to my husband.

We go to bed, and as I toss and turn, I make new plans for the next day.

The next day I wake up and I tell Kevin what I was going to do yesterday and that I am going to do it today. He runs ahead of me to take the pills away. It's ok; I will use a knife instead and I run to the draw, and he stops me.

I'm screaming, and crying.

He calls my psychiatrist, who tells him that he needs to take me to the ER to a "special hospital."

Kevin calls my friend Christine to help. She comes over and sits on the floor, and is telling me, as the tears flow down her face:

"It's time. It's time, Elaine, to get some help."

"Noooo! Don't take me away, if you take me away, I will never return."

Kevin and Christine manage to take me (more likely drag me) to the car. I didn't want to go. I thought they would inject me and put me to sleep.

Both Kevin and Christine ride in the car with me. Kevin is driving, Christine is in the front, and I am in the back, crying that I didn't want to go.

We arrive at ER. The waiting room is full. Kevin goes to the reception to give my details. Less than one minute later, I am called. Now I know that I was classed as a high priority. Have you ever been in any ER and try to understand why some people arrive after you but go in before you? It's because the receptionist is basically triaging by the questions she/he asks. If you are deemed to be in a critical condition, you will go ahead of others.

So here I go off to see the doctor. This is the beginning of a ten-day stay at a psychiatric unit that I lovingly refer to as "the resort."

Time in " The resort"

I'm taken in the ER to see a doctor. I'm asked to remove all my clothing, literally all my clothing, and put on scrubs. How humiliating to undress in front of strangers? I am also scanned to make sure that I have no metal on me; asked to squat and cough. I since learned this action is to remove any hidden drugs!

I go to meet my doctor. His assistant asks me a number of questions and I recall saying something about my God and her response being that this is what He wants for me. How crazy is that? How could He want me to be here?

All the time, Kevin and my friend Christine are sitting with me. The assistant leaves and I wait for the doctor. I recall sitting on the chair with one leg down and one leg on the top of the chair, and playing with the cord from the trouser leg. I am telling both of them that I am not staying and I am going home. They don't say anything but smile.

The doctor comes in, and once again I tell him that my God doesn't want me to be here. He tells me that God is everywhere – I question whether or not he is a believer. He is trying to convince me that I could go and stay in a new facility. It is like a resort, very nice. I laugh at him. I say:

"Do you think I'm stupid? I know what you are trying to do, you are trying to put me away, and I'm not going. I'm going home with my husband."

He calms me down and asks my husband to come and see him outside. I later learned that he was asking my husband questions and getting his agreement that I needed to go somewhere to get help, as I was a danger to myself. I will let Kevin tell you more about this in the section he has to share his story.

Kevin returns with the doctor. This time, Kevin is trying to convince me to go. Why would he do this? Doesn't he love me? I'm ok now; yes, it was stupid what I tried to do. I won't do it again. I promise!

This time the doctor takes my friend Christine outside to ask her questions. Afterwards, I learned that he was wanting to hear her side of the story. I will let Christine tell you more in the section she has to share.

We seem to spend forever in the doctor room. When are they going to let me go home? I request to go to the bathroom. Christine is allowed to come with me. As I walk to the toilet, I see people slowly walking around with blankets on their shoulders. I gesture to Christine that they look like they are crazy! She since told me that I looked like I was in a worse place. Funny but sad.

Returning from the bathroom, the doctor had spoken to both Kevin and Christine. Again, the doctor is trying to convince me to go to the "resort." Although I have told him that I didn't want to go, he basically tells me that I was going to go. They lead me out of the room and I am followed by Christine.

I hear the people walking with me say "court papers." I look at Christine and question why they are talking court papers. She told me it is nothing to think about. I am taken back into the room to get my belongings. Christine is looking through the door. I see the tears rolling down her face. I have no idea of what is happening to me.

A lady leads me to the car and puts me in the back. It looks like a regular town car. It has a window between the back seat and front seat, kind of like a taxi. I'm getting a taxi to the "resort." Of course, it's not a resort! That would be wishful thinking.

I sit in the back of the car. The lady asks me what music I wanted to hear. Christian music (of course) I reply. I turn to look out of the window and see Kevin and Christine. They are in Kevin's truck side by side with me. I look out of the window and I am trying to speak to Kevin.

"What's going on? Where are they taking me?"

Poor Kevin, he must have been as scared as I was.

We arrive at the resort. The driver calls ahead and the garage door is raised. We are the only car that arrives. The door rolls down behind us and I am let out of the car and met by a police officer. The first thing I say to him,

"What do I need to do to get out of here?"

I quickly learn that seems to be the one question that every guest in the resort asks. The response that normally comes from staff – focus on getting healthy and then you will be able to leave.

Similar to when you arrive at a resort, you have to go to reception and register. Registration at this resort is quite different. I enter the registration area and I am patted down, and photos taken. I feel like a criminal. I understand later that pictures of the body are taken as soon as you arrive to capture if there are any bruises or anything noticeable or unnoticeable. I guess it's to cover their backs in case anything happens whilst at the resort. Funny that when I left, no other pictures were taken.

Once I am registered, I go to the open area. It is visiting time, which means that Kevin and Christine are able to come in. The people in the visitor area look like the people in the hospital that I had just left; people walking around with blankets over their shoulders. I comment to Christine about the way people look. She laughs and says: "They look more normal than you." I know she is trying to bring some light humor.

I wait to be shown to my room. It is great! I have my own room. At least I didn't have to share my room with anyone. There is one single bed, a desk, and ensuite bathroom: quite the single resort room. The one difference is the bathroom.

There is no towel rail, and anything you could hold onto is filled in. I am told that this is to stop you from taking your life by using the rails to kill yourself. Toiletries and such things are held in a locker in the hallway. You have to ask the person at "reception" for the key. I assume this is the way of keeping control of what is being used.

The first night is quite challenging. Another guest has attempted to leave. I could hear bells ringing and lots of raucous. What am I doing here?

I manage to get some sleep; however, I notice at regular periods staff would stop by and look through the window in the door. Now they certainly don't do this in resorts. I imagine that I am in prison. The staff members are checking in like they do in prisons. I later learn this is something that they did to ensure nothing is happening in the bedrooms, and that guests are keeping themselves safe.

Six am arrives. During my ten-day stay at the resort, I get used to the "wake up call." It is the sound of the medical trolley moving from one room to the next. The nurse is checking vitals, giving any medication, and asking the same round of questions each day.

"Did you sleep well?" "How are you doing?" Of course, the answers to the questions are "Yes," and "I'm fine."

I am thinking if I tell them what I think they want to hear, then I will be able to get out of here quickly.

After checking vitals, then it's time to line up and go to breakfast. Yes, you read it, line up. Now this is where it really begins to feel less like a resort and more like a prisoner. We all line up for breakfast outside the common area. There are only about twenty of us – quite the boutique resort. A staff member leads us; the police officer that greeted me at the welcome desk in the garage is the last person in line.

This is the first time that I really "communicated" with any of the guests. People are curious about when I arrived. And most people would then ask, "When are you getting out?" How did I know; all I want is to get out as soon as I was able.

Breakfast is surprisingly very healthy, lots of choices, and the service is fantastic. Interestingly, I choose the same breakfast each day, a yogurt and some oatmeal. It seems the safe option to me. The doctor in ER is correct; it is like a resort.

I collect my breakfast and go through the checkout, except there is no money exchanged. Is this an attempt to make you feel "normal," or simply their way of keeping inventory?

Now where do I sit? Everyone seems to have their cliques. I'm looking around to see some "normal" friendly faces. I wonder what I must have looked like to the others?

A lady gestures me over to her table. I sit with her and a few others. I recall a guy who shared his story that he had been in and out of the resorts and was now waiting to hear when he was moving onto the next one. Really? Why is he not getting any other help? Of course, I don't know his entire story.

It amazes me to hear other guests' stories. Everyone is pretty open about how many times they have tried to kill themselves; what medications they are taking; and the impact of the different drugs as the doctors tried to determine what was best for them. Some of them even sound quite proud of their stories, while others not so much.

People I Recall Meeting at the Resort

A lady who is Sunday school teacher: She has signed herself into the resort because she knows she needs to "balance her meds" (using her words). Why on earth would you come check yourself into this resort of all places? She was a Sunday school teacher. I gravitate towards spending time with her. She was prepping for her class next Sunday and knew she was here for a set period of time. I have no idea how long I would be here for.

Two other women lived in my area and they are here because of blood work results. I wonder how true that really is – I mean why would you put yourself in this place and volunteer?

It's amazing how much information you can learn from other guests. The staff are not going to give you what you are looking for. I share my story with guests and one told me that I could sign a form to say that I have "volunteered" to come here. Really? Why would I do that? Apparently if I sign the form, I can be out in seventy-two hours. I did it. This meant that I no longer had to go to court and I would later learn how vital it was I signed this form. Volunteering versus being committed makes such a big difference in so many ways. Thank you, Jesus, for introducing me to these guests.

More about a "typical" day. After breakfast, guests would go to their rooms or to the common room. It is a very scheduled day.

Session 1. Check in. We would all sit in a circle, except me. I would sit outside the circle at a table in the back of the room. The check-in is a way to meet other guests and learn about what their goals are and how we can all get along together.

Session 2. Group time with counsellors. Each guest is given a counsellor to work with individually. However, each day after checking in, we would have a lesson guided by the counsellor. These sessions are based on equipping us to become well and cover many different topics.

One session I recall the most is about the bird in the cage. I recall the cage is open; however, because the bird has been there so long, even with the cage open, it would stay there. The closest poem I found to what I recall is from Allen James:

> *The door to freedom opened,*
> *Yet there he still remained,*
> *For the will to fly has atrophied,*
> *And the bird is finally caged (Allen 2019)*

It very much relates to the power of the mind and how we can all be impacted by the way we capture our thoughts. I have done so much research and studying on the mind, brain, and body connection since, and it's fascinating the power of the mind.

Session 3. Break. Snacks and drinks – are they looking for us to put on weight?

Session 4. Individual meeting with doctor. Remember back I had mentioned my friend told me not to talk about God. The doctor is accompanied with my personal counsellor. They ask:

"Do I see people?"

"No."

"Do I hear voices?"

"No. Other than the conversations that I have with God and Satan." I'm a faithful Christian.

"Do I want to kill myself?"

"No," even if I still thought I was not going to admit it to the doctor. Of course, they already thought I was unstable, as I was having conversations with God and Satan.

"Do I want to commit homicide (killing others)?"

"No."

So, it's all good, right – this is a good session? Clearly not; I am not going anywhere anytime soon. However, I have started to take my medication. I have to because the nurse would wait until I have swallowed the pill.

Lunch time. Same process. Line up and go to lunch. Great food. I ate veggie burgers most days. The choices are always good. Once we go through the "checkout," time to choose who to sit with. I gravitate to the same people at the same table. It's amazing how important routine becomes.

After lunch – one-on-one time with counsellor. This seems more like a friendly conversation. Of course, he is extremely skilled in having a conversation to learn about what's going on in my mind. I really don't recall too many of the conversations. The most recalled ones follow:

Conversations with resort counsellor

I am sitting in the open lounge, listening in on a group session. I am sitting at my chair at the table in the back of the room and with a pencil, I am digging this into my leg; drawing pictures and really digging in the lead. I couldn't feel anything. I am looking into the reception area. I know the staff are looking in. Of course, they will be observing us. Next, I notice my counsellor inviting me for a walk outside.

We are walking in the "courtyard"; this area was used as part of our daily exercise. The image in my mind is like a prison exercise yard. The guests would all walk round in a circle. Some would connect and some would be alone.

Here I am walking the yard with my counsellor. I recall asking him did he read the Bible. Of course, he says he has. I am telling him how I could not leave this place; how I would be without a job, a home, and nothing. He is trying his best to help me think why I thought that way. I am sharing Bible parables with him. I tell him how I thought I was the young rich ruler, the thorn in the bush. He asks me questions about how ready I felt to go home. "I'm ready. Whenever you are ready to let me go, I'm ready."

Another experience with my counsellor is when I have a meltdown before dinner. I feel like I could not move and I could not go into dinner. I am terrified. He is encouraging me to come into dinner and help me see reality, but it isn't working at all. Eventually, he is "pulling me" to dinner. He did a great job of "encouraging" me to go sit at dinner.

I learn that the counsellors work seven days on and seven days off. I really connected with my counsellor and have gotten to the point where I felt like I am ready to go home. Well not really, I want them to think I am ready to go, so that I could go and kill myself.

It is a Saturday and I know the counsellor is getting ready to finish his shift. I didn't want to let him down. The doctor and the counsellor are asking me about my readiness. I want to convince them I am ready. I did tell my counsellor that I couldn't verbalize what I had in my mind. My thing is that if I say it out loud, it would become real. I want to write it down.

I take a piece of paper and write my thoughts. My thought is that if I had spoken to a psychiatrist, then I would be going to hell. It is really hard for me to write that. I hold the pencil tightly and I'm sure my writing is illegible.

I have told my husband that I am fooling the doctor, and my counsellor and I am telling them lies in order to "get out."

My husband has a conversation with the staff. I am so excited that I am ready to go home.

I am taken back into my room to have the conversation about going home. The counsellor tells me, "We have come to the decision and you are not going home."

"What!" I can't believe what he is saying.

"I'm not going home, why not?"

I later learned that my husband had told them I was not being truthful and I was trying to fool them. My husband had my back; it was a real act of love from him. He could have been selfish and agree with me, and help me "get out." But he cared enough to keep me in the resort.

After that weekend, my counsellor left for his seven-day break and also did my doctor. Doctors also worked a seven- on and a seven-off.

So, I am staying here for a little while longer.

Back to the "typical day" and stories of the guests and events.

The days are mixed with group sessions, individual sessions, food – breakfast, lunch, dinner, and morning, afternoon, and evening snacks.

Some of the group exercises included walking the courtyard, going into the gym. Staff and guests would play basketball. There is corn hole. I really thought deep about cornhole. The red and the blue items that you throw into the hole, I was thinking that blue was God and red was Satan! In my mind, at that time there, was a real competition between both of these "people." It still feels quirky this day to play corn hole.

I tended to keep myself and didn't feel like part of the group. I didn't want to be part of the group. All these people were amazing. My heart goes out to all these broken people and I pray each one of them has found peace.

I would sit on the exercise bike, not really doing much but it just gives me an opportunity to be alone. I know that in all these situations the staff are observing us. I can imagine them going back to their offices and doing briefings on each of their "guests."

Even when we went to walk and went to exercise, we would have to line up, just like we would need to do when going to breakfast and dinner. It is in these moments that I felt like I was in prison, especially as some people would wear their scrubs. I would wear regular clothes as my way of feeling normal, except that I am not allowed laces in my sneakers. Who knows what I would do with a set of laces?

We also have "free" time. At free time, some people color, others do jigsaw puzzles, whilst others sit and watch TV. I still struggle these days to color and do jigsaw puzzles.

I had only been there a few days when the TV announced the death of Robin Williams. Robin Williams had surprisingly taken his life by suicide. The media was all over the fact about how could he possibly have done this given the nature of the personality. It took me back to the time when I shared my testimony at church and people came and shared that they could not believe what I had done, because I seemed like I had it all together. My response:

"I am human and susceptible. None of us are safe from this." There is a verse in the Bible that Satan comes to steal kill, and destroy. He roams around. If we let him in, it's challenging if we are weak (1 Pet. 5:8).

Today, I still wonder why the resort kept the TV channels showing with the Robin Williams story. Why would they do that? Would it give people in the resort some tips?

It was very interesting the way the longer I stayed in the resort, the more it seemed like home. It became a safe haven. Why would I want to go out into the big, bad world? Now that is really crazy thinking! However, I still did "crazy" things. As I look back, I think about the times I was alone in my "ensuite." I would literally have conversations with myself in the mirror.

"Oh, my Elaine, what are you doing here, what has become of you?"

All this time I was still planning to get out so I could kill myself. I couldn't believe it when I had the opportunity to do so in the resort.

I had started my period! Yup! Crazy – how could this possibly happen? Well, I suppose because I am a woman and that's what happens to us on a regular basis! I had to go to the front desk to ask for some supplies. They generously gave me a few. This is it! I know, let's see if I can kill myself with a tampon! Yes, you read it, a tampon!

I stood in the bathroom and was looking at myself in the mirror, mouth open trying to put it in my throat. Of course, as it gets moist with my saliva, it expands. There is no way this is going down my throat so I give up. Never mind, I will be out here soon and I will be able to complete the task.

A few times the doctor would ask me if I was ready to leave the resort. I would say of course, but for some reason, I was still there. Guess the insurance agreed to continue to make the payments!

What follows next are the events that I recall from my stay at the resort.

Other Stories from The Resort

Young fainting lady. The guests at the resort were of all ages. There was a young lady who had been homeless and ended up here after trying to kill herself many times. It's interesting how everyone seems to have tried to end it all, not just me. How many others are out there feeling the same way, doing the same thing because they feel shameful or hopeless? If that's you and you are reading this, I encourage you to reach out to someone, a doctor, a friend. You are not alone and you can get help. Drop the pride and the feeling that no one cares – go ahead and pick up the phone, text or call – you can do it.

This young lady did it. She reached out for help and received the care she needed. She was even helped when she fainted at breakfast one morning. We were all sitting, "enjoying" our meals. Next minute, thud! She was on the floor. The staff came around and helped her. She got help immediately. All is good.

Young man who thought **he had been dropped out of heaven.** The day I checked in the resort and was waiting in reception at visitor hours, there was a young man with lots of visitors. I learned they were his girlfriend and also others, including his church pastor. The young man seemed in quite a state. He would constantly cry out to God and ask for forgiveness; this was a daily occurrence. Sometimes he was kept in his room, as he was unsafe. I learned that he thought he had died and gone to heaven; however, for some reason, God had dropped him back. He wanted to be in heaven. His family and friends visited him daily. One day, there were no more cries and we learned that he had been moved to another place, probably got an upgrade to another resort.

The joyful trans. A guy who dressed as a lady would be constantly happy and trying to share joy. He/she would have long hair and painted nails (not sure how he/she had access to the nail paint). He/she was hilarious in the fact that he would only respond when the female name was used. He had some quite interesting stories – which I will choose to refrain from sharing. One never knows who may be reading the book.

My visit from Satan. This was a really scary/weird/surreal moment. One day, a new guy turned up and had a security guard with him. The guard would be with him at all times. We would go for our daily walks, and for some reason the guy took a liking to me. On the walk, he would speaking to me strangely and told me he had been called to spend time with me and that we were related. Seriously! I knew it; I knew I was in Satan's family! (of course, that is so far from the truth. I am a child of God! And I stand firm on that truth.) He called me Barbara and, silly me, told him my real name. So, he continued to call on me.

We went back into the reception / day room after the walk for a group session. He sat next to me. I noticed he had Bible verses on his forearm, then he rolled up his sleeve to show me the top of his arm, and that tattoo was a skeleton. Creepy. I felt scared.

Next thing I knew the police officer was calling me out. He wanted to know if the guy was bothering me. Heck yes, he was. My "friends" commented that he had taken quite the liking to me. Oh my!

It was so weird he was there for that short moment in time; before I knew it, he had disappeared. They made an assessment that he had to be in a different place. Thank you, Jesus.

By this stage, the doctors and counsellors had changed shift.

The new female doctor had a different style. She didn't have a friendly bedside manner. Nope, you had to go see her in her office. The day that "Satan came to visit," I described this event to the new doctor. I told her not to write anything down. Of course, she was going to afterwards, even though she told me she wouldn't. I know I must have sounded crazy writing this. I think that sounded crazy! Well not at that moment; it all seemed so real to me.

Along with the counsellors changing (Doug, my first counsellor left), I was given a new counsellor. She didn't seem as connected as Doug. It must be hard for these people. I had built a relationship and now I had to build a new relationship. The previous doctor told, and Doug would tell me, that the statistics were that a person would stay on average "at the resort" for five to seven days. I kept thinking of that key performance indicator. I didn't want to skew the statistics; I needed to get out of here and soon.

I went through the same process with the counsellor, answering the same questions. Do you see anything, do you hear anything, blah, blah!!

Part of the process of trying to measure progress was to complete an action plan of readiness.

I would complete the action plan based on what I thought the resort staff wanted to see. I thought I could trick the system! Well, I had tried that once before but my husband foiled that plan. I'm not going to tell him anything anymore. He may betray me again!

My new counsellor lasted about three days; however, she had vacation and so I was given a different counsellor. I didn't appreciate it; however, I was thinking it would work in my favor. I didn't have time to build up a relationship and they didn't get time to learn about me.

I was determined to get out of here and was playing the game, answering the questions with what I thought they expected to hear from a "well person."

The daily routines continued. The bleeping of the machines in the morning to test vitals, breakfast, the group sessions, break time, walk in the courtyard, lunch time, activities, break time, "free time," dinner, visiting time, evening snacks, medication before going to bed, sleep, and start all over again.

I looked forward to visiting hours. Both Kevin and Christine would visit. Kevin was continuing to do his soccer coaching, so Christine would take the "first shift" and then when Kevin arrived, she would leave us to be alone. It was so nice they would make the journey to come see me. The resort was in the country, away from where I lived. I am forever grateful to both of them. I felt so sorry for those people who didn't have regular visitors. If you are reading this book and you have someone in the hospital for any reason, I would strongly encourage you to arrange with family, friends, church members, whomever you can, to visit those in need. This is super important to know that someone will be there. I can't even begin to imagine what it must have been like to be sitting alone, in an already depressed state, and see others being visited. Please, I cannot stress how important it is.

I'm sure it took a toll on both of them to make the trip and sit with me daily. I will let them tell their side of the story in the section dedicated to them.

I specifically recall a visit when both Kevin and Christine were with me at the same time. I was more stressed than normal, as I had determined in this visit I was going to make a confession. About twenty-five years previously, while still in England and before we knew Christ, I had been unfaithful. I know that I was forgiven by my God, and I know that

I was cleansed by His blood. BUT I had told Christine several years previous and I still felt bad that I had not told Kevin. I wanted to be sure that there were no secrets; that Satan wouldn't have anything on me that he could keep a hold of me. (Well, I don't think I was thinking that clearly, at the time, as to the reason why I wanted to share.) All I know is that I had a burning desire to share my dark secret with Kevin.

I kept telling Kevin I had something to share. He was encouraging me to do so. On the other hand, Christine was encouraging me to keep silent. She was scared that this may be the breaking point for Kevin. I just sat with Kevin, holding his hands and crying, telling him I needed to share something. Christine stood up and walked away. I told Kevin that I had been unfaithful. Phew! What a relief. Then he shared he had also been unfaithful at the same time! Bastard! How could he have done that to me? Now I was unsure. In hindsight, it was the best confession that both of us could have made to each other. There were, and are, no more dark secrets that Satan can take a hold of us.

In hindsight, this was a big chain broken.

Back to the schedule….After visiting hours were snacks, free time, medication, and sleep.

The night nurse came to your bed, asked you a few questions, took your vitals, watched you take your medication, and then off to sleep.

I had created a plan. I was going to "act normal" so that I could get out. This one evening, I decided to distract the nurse by having a conversation with her, and distract her from giving me my medication. It worked; I missed the medication. I was telling her how normal I felt and how ready I was to go home.

The next day with my third counsellor, I went through the motions of "acting normal" to go through my action plan when I was to leave the resort. Next was to have the conversation with the doctor.

Not sure how the decision was made, but they told me I could leave. What a relief. I was so happy. I could get out and finally kill myself.

Kevin was contacted and we made arrangements. The news spread quickly. I was getting to leave. It had been ten long days. I had connected with some people, and it felt weird to be leaving this safe place. We collected my belongings. As I sat in the car, I really didn't feel ready to leave – had I done the right thing? I had access to my cell phone. I picked it up. It felt so strange; it was like the first time I had seen one. Everything felt so surreal. Having come from a very structured environment to no structure felt odd. Where are my snacks, etc.?

We got home and I wanted to play a game. Isn't that what normal people do? I played Mastermind with Kevin. Crazy!! While playing the game, I shared with him that I felt I really didn't love him and don't think I had ever loved him. What? Where did that come from? This man had been through hell and back with me, and I throw that at him. Clearly, I was not fully well. He told me later that for all that he had experienced, that was the toughest moment for him. Thankfully we got through that moment and at the time of writing this book, we have been married for thirty-five years. I am reminded what he said to me at the start of this crazy summer. He said, "Elaine, for better or worse, in sickness or health, until death do, we part." I love you so much, Kevin, and am forever grateful. To this day, I refer to you as my hero.

I was home now. What next? Little did I know that I was not going to be totally free. Instead of leaving the resort to go home, the next part of my journey I refer to as going to the "spa"; an outpatient facility that I had to go to daily for three weeks!

The "Spa"

Saturday arrived: my first day of "freedom." I had no idea what to do. I'm sure Kevin was wary of leaving me alone. So, we hung out together. In the evening, there was "music in the park." I think a lot of towns/cities have these events when the weather is nice. It's a way of bringing families and friends together, to chill out, play games, drink wine, have picnics, and listen to free music.

We went to a local event, and it was so weird. There were fall clothes in the shops. I felt like I had missed an entire season, where had the time gone? We grab something to eat and stayed to listen to the music.

All the time we are standing there, I was thinking about my next steps in how I could kill myself. On the outside, I looked "normal." I had conversations with passersby. I smiled and joked. But all the time, the thoughts in my mind were not normal.

Sunday came and we decided to go to church. I wanted to sneak in and stay at the back. I felt such shame. I didn't want to be around people who knew what had happened. I really just wanted to curl up and go in a corner. We stayed at the back and I clung onto Kevin for dear life. It was so difficult to praise and worship. I wasn't feeling very intimate with the Lord at that point in time. I do know, however, that he was with me through every step of the way.

The weekend passed and it was time to go to the spa. I had to drag myself out of bed. I really didn't want to go anywhere else. I knew I had to and really didn't have any choice. Kevin was very loving and encouraged me to go.

The spa was in a place known as the cottages. There was an intake process, which thankfully was nothing like the intake process at the resort. My husband and I had to answer a few questions with my "social worker." I then got to meet my doctor, whose care I would be under for the next three weeks.

The doctor told me I had been dismissed from the resort with a diagnosis of psychotic major depressive disorder! What, "psychotic"? I really didn't want that to be on my records. I may have been depressed but certainly not psychotic. It took me some time later to understand that my "conversations with God and Satan" – which, by the way, is very normal for a Christian and child of God – were likely the reason for the diagnosis. This was confirmed after my conversation with the spa doctor. He told me he was going to take the word "psychotic" off the records, as he understood that was more to do with my spiritual beliefs. Thank you, Jesus, one more time.

After my intake, I was taken into the "class." The conference room had approximately fifteen guests. Some had been visiting the spa for varying lengths of time and I was the new person.

Basically, the way the days were structured at the spa, we would start off with breakfast. It's amazing how much you get fed. Guess though for some that was the way they got their basic need of food taken care of.

After breakfast – for which we did not have to line up or have a police officer taking us to and from the cafeteria – we went to class. We would be in class learning about a topic, talking about our feelings, and then off to lunch.

I was able to connect with a few people in my class for lunch. Each day I would eat the same food and sit with the same people. Even though the first day I thought "Why am I in here with these people?" I didn't fully appreciate I needed the help just as much as they did.

After lunch, we would have another session and then finish around 2:30-ish. Kevin would come and pick me up from the spa and then we would go for a walk around the mall. It was too hot to be outside. To this day, it still feels weird to walk around the mall.

You may recall I was a facilitator before the start of my crazy summer. In fact, I am a professional facilitator, which means I am the worst student to have in your class, as I will be super critical – well, at these classes with my fixed mindset. I was probably a nightmare for the facilitators – although in saying that I'm sure I was not the worst student they had.

I will share my poor behavior for which I am not proud. If anyone is reading this book from the places that care for people with mental health issues, I raise my hands to you and want to give you a huge hug for your patience and care.

Bad behavior

The facilitator would pass out handouts. We would have to each take turns at reading parts of the handouts and then having a discussion. Why do this? I felt like I was at school! Why not give us the handouts to take home, read, and then come prepared for an active discussion? Duh! Who would have actually read the handouts and come prepared for a discussion? Most of us were not even thinking clearly! Of course, to read in the class actually meant we would read it.

Gestalt. The facilitator asks, "Who knows Gestalt theory?" I raised my hand. I literally had this topic in one of the classes I had previously facilitated a few months previous. Although I was thankful he didn't ask me to explain, as I really could only remember the title at that point in time! However, in my mind I was thinking, "I should be up there facilitating this session. I would make it a lot more interactive!" I would ask the facilitator questions to try to trip him up.

Video player: After lunch one day, the facilitator wanted us to watch a video of someone sharing their story. Not sure why they do this, but maybe to give us hope that the stories they share are all about people who come through their problems. Guess so, however hopeful was not what I was feeling at that point in time.

She kept playing with the VHS – yes, a VHS, not even a DVD player! The system was so underfunded. Who used VHS these days? She was definitely having issues with loading and playing the video. Now if this happened in a class that I was a participant in today, I would be very empathetic and out myself in their shoes and offer to assist. Nope, that was not me when I was in the class. Instead of helping, I said out loud, "Any decent facilitator would have tested their equipment and be all ready to go before class started." Ouch! Every time I think of that, I cringe. I am so sorry.

With my social worker, I would have conversations about my goals and coping mechanisms. Of course, I would tell them what they wanted to hear, although I was still adamant that I would not be able to go back into the workforce or even get a job as a greeter!

I recall that one time she said to me, "Are you always this stubborn?" I don't know, am I? I was not happy with this change process.

It was interesting in the spa, as guests would come and go. Similar to the resort, I would make a deeper connection with some more than others.

Some Memorable Outpatient Friends

Linda. She was African–American. My heart hurt for her. She had been in and out of homelessness since the age of nine. She had tried to kill herself multiple times. I wonder how the system was really caring for her. She had the most amazing, gentle nature and seemed so caring. It's funny how of all the people I met, I can only remember Linda's name.

There was a Caucasian lady who told me she had been in and out of these places several times. She had even experienced electric shock treatment. Oh my, I couldn't even imagine.

Each day, I would hang out with these ladies and become more connected. The time was going by. When was I going to be let go?

Each day started the same. Kevin would "encourage" me to go on the elliptical machine to get some exercise. I pictured myself slumped over the machine, barely able to use the machine. I'm sure every little bit helped.

I was also at the point where I drove myself to and from the spa. Yay, I was at least getting some freedom. I guess I could have actually decided not to go to the sessions, but I was "called" there. Actually, even though I did have a choice, I didn't feel at that point in time that I did.

At the end of each day, we would go around the mall, or to the park if the weather wasn't too hot.

Each day, I kept taking my medication.

The three weeks were almost up. I was counting down the days until I could go on the cruise.

Now the cruise is not a phrase that I am using for another facility. It is actually a cruise that I had booked a year previous, as we wanted to go and visit our daughter as she was celebrating her thirtieth birthday, and we had invited my next-door neighbor as a gift for her 80th birthday. It was so God that the time from leaving the resort to leaving the spa to going on the cruise was exactly three weeks: the length of time for my stay at the spa. God is so in the details. It meant that I didn't have any spare time between the spa and cruise where I would be alone. Who knows I may have tried to kill myself again? That was still on my mind.

When your time is up at the spa, you get to graduate! Graduation means that you have met your goals and you are ready to leave. Again, I felt like I had played the system, as I did not really feel I was ready, but I just wanted to get out, go on the cruise, and then kill myself. Yes, I was still thinking this.

Graduation day! As well as getting a certificate and resources to take with you, everyone in the room had the opportunity to say a few words of encouragement.

I recall Linda had a big smile and reminded me that she was going to miss me eating saltine crackers each day for lunch. Others made reference to missing my English accent.

The most amazing message was from a guy who had only been in the spa for five days. You may recall that people came in and out of the class at different times, depending on when they were "invited" to the spa. This guy said the following words:

"I know I haven't been here that long, and we haven't really got to know each other, but I have five words for you. 'Let go and let God.'"

You have got to be kidding me. If you recall at the start of the book, I talk about my journey going through Grace Life International Training to be a Christian counsellor and the title of my final paper was: Let go and let God. It still gives me chills when I recall this. If that wasn't a clear message, I don't know what was – even though there had been many messages. However, I was still not fully healed and even though it touched me then, it has made more of an impact since.

September 2014 - The Cruise

I graduated on a Friday, and the next day we were setting off for a cruise. We had to fly to Barcelona, Spain to pick up the ship. How could I possibly make that journey? How could I get on a plane? How could I be around people in an airport? It caused me great anxiety. I tried to convince myself that it would be ok. This was something that I did all the time for the previous years. Getting on a plane was almost like getting on a bus for me. A plane ride is my commute to work. For those of you who are reading who are management consultants, or in a job where you are regularly on the road, I am sure you can relate.

Was this the start of my thinking beginning to shift? I didn't think so. All I knew was that I was going on this cruise with the one goal to spend time with my daughter and son-in-law so that I could say "good-bye," come home, and kill myself!

On the cruise, I acted quite "normal." I was the life and soul of the party. I made friends with people. It was quite fun, except for poor Kevin. When we got back to the room, I would turn and be quite nasty to him.

I wanted to tell Angela and Rodrigo about what had happened, and wondered when would be the best time. At the start or at the end of the cruise? Each had different pros and cons. I figured it would happen when it was meant to happen. Wow! I am "letting go!"

The first night we had an opportunity to hang out with Angela, as Rodrigo was working in the photo studio. I plucked up the courage, took a deep breath, and told her about everything. She told me she already knew. Not only had my neighbor told her – we had not told her not to – she told me she had guessed what had happened. She wasn't able to send me any cards – I may use the sharp edges to do something and I was not allowed to speak to her when I was in the resort. She is not stupid. She has high intuition, just like her mum.

With that "announcement" out of the way, we were able to enjoy the rest of the cruise. I kept taking my medication.

The Sunday of the cruise came and it was time to leave to go home. As I write these next few sentences, I can only describe what felt like a switch being flicked on in my mind.

The Light Comes On

It was literally like a light switch had been flicked on in my mind. I felt well. I felt ready to go back to work. All was good with the world. How could this happen like this? What I didn't know is that the medication takes six to eight weeks to kick in. Being under care in the resort and spa, and having to be accountable to take my medication, had forced me to continue. The result was amazing. I felt like I was normal.

"Ok," I told Kevin, "I'm ready to go back to work." What? Wait? I had an appointment with my psychologist that Tuesday. I told her I was ready to go back to work. I may need some marriage counselling; however, I was no longer afraid to go back to work. She told me I needed my psychiatrist to sign me back that I was medically fit. I apologized for the way I had treated her in the sessions. I'm sure I was not the first or last person that reacted the way I did. God bless the psychologists of this world.

Ok, off to the psychiatrist the next day. I walked in with a big smile on my face. I sat down in the same chair I always sat on. You may recall I didn't want to sit on the sofa. I boldly said: "I'm ready to go back to work. Please sign and give me permission to go back, with no restrictions, full-time." He asked me a few questions. He didn't seem surprised that I was ready to go. I guess he was familiar with the situation of the light switch coming on after a certain period of time.

We talked about my journey. I told him that I was upset at first because I knew he didn't know God, and he wanted me not to focus there. His response surprised me. He said:

"How do you know I don't believe in God? My job is to help you get well. Sometimes people with a strong faith are hindered by this and it is my job to help you through this."

Wow, that was quite a turn-up for the books. I thanked him for all the time that we were together, and hope that respectfully I would not see him again.

I left the doctor's office and went to pay my bill. Finally, my receipt showed that I am "back to normal." I didn't have to pay much for that visit. It had been a costly process. Thank you, Jesus, that I had the benefit of short- term disability and was able to be paid while I was absent.

As I got ready to check out, there was a lady checking in for the first time with her husband supporting her. I had a flashback to the start of my journey in this place: how I didn't feel like I should be there, and how the doctor was not going to help me. Now several months later, I was happy, ready to go to work, and full of joy. I paid my bill and went over to the lady. She was in such a mess. I asked for her permission to speak to her. The one piece of advice I gave her:

"Please, whatever you do, listen to the doctor. Take your medication. It took me a long time to get healthy, and it would have been a lot quicker if I had sought help sooner, and took my medication."

She looked at me and smiled a small smile, and nodded her head. I'm not sure how much she heard and listened to the advice. However, when she was called into the doctor's office, I heard her scream and break down crying. At least she took her husband in. I pray that whoever you are that you are now in a healthy place. My message to all who may be feeling the same way is to listen to the doctor. Now, of course, I don't know your individual situation, and my doctor has given her words of advice at the front of the book. I would encourage you not to rule it out.

I had decided I was ready to go back to work. I really didn't know what that meant. I reached out to everyone I needed, but how was I going to turn up, after being away for what felt like six months, and act "normal"?

Again, God is in the details. The office I was working at was going through a remodeling. The Friday of the same week that I had arrived from the cruise, they were hosting an open house of the new layout. It was open to family members. Yes! I could take Kevin with me and he could help me navigate the conversations.

In my role as a consultant, I would travel a lot, and so it was not unusual for me to be away from the office for long periods of time. When people saw me, and made comments like, "Hey, I haven't seen you in a while," I would simply smile and not say a whole lot.

My psychologist had given me some coaching on how to respond in these situations. What I realized is that when people ask questions in these moments, like: "How are you doing?" or "What have you been up to?" they really are not looking for a lot of information. It is pretty surface level, which meant that I didn't have to give a full response. Phew! I got through the open house. Now to prepare to go back on Monday.

Monday, I drove to the office. Step 1 check. We have a "hot desk, hoteling" set-up, which means you don't have the same desk allocated to you. It works out really well, especially given that consultants are very rarely in their own office, as they are constantly travelling. I found a desk to sit at – step 2 check.

I started to make phone calls and reach out to people. It felt really weird. I make it through the day and drove home. Step 3 check.

I was now in the process of finding my next piece of work. I didn't want to go back to my previous consulting role. It was only within a couple of weeks that I secured an internal role, which meant no travel and working from home. Thank you, Jesus. It is amazing though how I got this role – of course because God was all over it.

The back story to this. Several years ago, when I was in my training role, I was asked to facilitate a meeting for a team. This meant that I had to stay in Chicago an extra day. I was scheduled to do a three-hour slot at the meeting. However, like many meetings, each session ran over. I had ninety minutes to do my session. It was amazing that I finished right on the dot of ninety minutes. I was able to connect really well with the team and their leader. Fast forward a couple of years later.

I was scrolling the job board and came across a role that looks like it had my name written all over it – even if it was a staff level above my current role. I called the recruiter and she told me that the recruiting manager was the leader of the team I had facilitated the meeting for years ago. Well, she will either love me or not!

I spoke with the leader, flew up to NYC for an interview, and I was given the job.

During this time, I was thinking about my next steps. I had a choice. I could either live in shame and in the darkness, or I could fight evil with good and use my situation to bring hope and light to others. I was not going to walk around with a banner or post it on a billboard:

"Hey everyone, I tried to kill myself. I attempted suicide!"

No, I was going to be light to others. This was first confirmed when I went to get a new radio for my car. I was speaking to the store owner and commented on the fact that they had signs with Christian quotes on the walls. He told me he could do this, as it was a private business and he had more freedom. We got talking. For some unknown reason, he started telling me about his wife and how she was unwell, and she needed to take medication. Wow! Ok here I go.

I shared that I understand what she was going through. I began to share my story with him, and it felt so natural. He was inspired and it gave him hope. This is what I have been called to do; to bring light and hope. I fully subscribe to the thinking that it's a lot easier to coach / counsel / empathize with people if you have been in that place yourself. As I said earlier in the book, this is not a situation I would put on my worst enemy; however, I am very thankful that I was "chosen" to go through the experience.

Throughout my journey, several people shared the same story with me. Sometimes in my journey I would not accept it; however now, I get it.

The story goes like this:

A very old man was once caught in rising floodwaters. He climbed onto the roof of his house and trusted God to rescue him. A neighbour came by in a canoe and said, "The waters will soon be above your house. Hop in and we'll paddle to safety."

"No thanks," replied the religious man. "I've prayed to God and I'm sure he will save me."

A short time later, the police came by in a boat. "The waters will soon be above your house. Hop in and we'll take you to safety."

"No thanks," replied the religious man. "I've prayed to God and I'm sure he will save me."

A little time later, a rescue services helicopter hovered overhead, let down a rope ladder, and said, "The waters will soon be above your house. Climb the ladder and we'll fly you to safety."

"No thanks," replied the religious man. "I've prayed to God and I'm sure he will save me."

All this time the floodwaters continued to rise, until soon they reached above the roof and the religious man drowned. When he arrived at heaven, he demanded an audience with God. Ushered into God's throne room, he said, "Lord, why am I here in heaven? I prayed for you to save me, I trusted you to save me from that flood."

"Yes, you did, my child" replied the Lord. "And I sent you a canoe, a boat, and a helicopter. But you never got in."

God works in mysterious ways, and I have found that more often than not, the way He answers my prayers is very rarely like the way I expect. It took a trip to see a psychiatrist, a visit to a "resort" and "spa" for my prayers to be answered, where it would have been a lot easier for me to reach out and take the rope. Many times, God will give us the answer; we have to take action. "Faith without works is dead" (James 2: 14-26).

God uses other people. He equips doctors with the skills and knowledge required to help. I am very thankful for that. He even uses dogs!

You may recall earlier that year I was in Chicago and lost my precious dog – Snowy! Well, now that I am back in work, and in an internal role that required minimum travel, it was time to get a new dog.

I went to my vet's (that looked after Snowy) with the intent of seeking advice on where to go for a new dog. I wanted a rescue. As I walked in, there she was! Her foster owner had called her Patsy after Patsy Cline, because he names all his animals after country singers. As I write this, how apt for Patsy. What was one of Patsy Cline's record hits? CRAZY! Well if that wasn't a sign, I don't know what is.

Patsy had been left in a box on the corner of the road. The foster owner was bringing her in to be checked out. I expressed my desire to own Patsy. However, she was already tagged to a family. The family had first right of refusal.

Patsy only lasted a day in her new home. Apparently, the owner had children and Patsy doesn't like children. To this day, she doesn't like children getting in her face.

I had to change the name; I couldn't call her Patsy. Short aside, my next-door neighbor in Florida is called Patsy. I always wanted to call Snowy Simba, out of the Lion King, still one of my all-time favourite movies. Patsy is, of course, female and so I called her Kiara. Kiara is Simba's daughter.

To this day, I still refer to Kiara in this way: "Kiara rescued me and I rescued her."

She has been such an amazing dog. I would fully attribute the fact to having a dog as a help in my recovery. They are like children and need looking after, except unlike children they never grow up! If you recall in my crazy summer, I isolated myself and didn't have Snowy to keep me company.

There is power in community, even if it is a dog.

PART 3: The Power of Support

Exodus 17:12 (ESV): "But Moses' hands grew weary, so they took a stone and put it under him, and he sat on it, while Aaron and Hur held up his hands, one on one side, and the other on the other side. His hands were steady until the going down of the sun."

In the Bible, it gives many examples of friends being there for each other. I like the above reference. If Moses lowered his hands, then the enemy would be winning; however, with the support of his friends keeping his arms raised, his army was able to defeat the enemy.

The power of having a support system, no matter how small, cannot be underestimated. Throughout my story, I have mentioned my God, my family, my friends, my work colleagues. This next section is devoted to two people without whom I would not still be here today.

My hero, my husband – Kevin. My best friend, prayer partner – Christine. I will also share some insight to other friends who made a difference. The previous pages were written from my perspective.

The following pages may sound familiar; however, you will see that the way I saw what was happening was quite different to my supporters. You will find their perspectives interesting and different.

My Husband's Perspective

My husband Kevin was my rock through the crazy summer. He is my hero. On a ride home from the beach, I "interviewed" him to share his perspective. This chapter is created to represent the "interview."

Me: Tell me about the night that I came home from the client and I told you that I wanted to quit my job. I remember you met me as usual at the airport, always with a cup of tea, wearing clothes that you had changed into. You always like to show up "smart" for me – I love that you do that, even though you know I love you regardless what you are wearing.

Kevin: When you got into the car, the song "Happy" was the playing on the radio. You told me to switch it off and was telling me that you couldn't do this anymore and had to quit your job. I was obviously concerned about this.

I knew this was not like you. You loved your job, and you were the main breadwinner, which was not an issue for me because we both loved our jobs. I knew you were having a tough time with the guy on the project. But that was not unusual. I remember when you first joined your company that it was stressful for you. It still "scares" me when I hear you coughing or "baulking," as that is how your stress showed up in the early years. So, this wasn't about the person or the job; it was something more.

You kept telling me that you were going to send an email to your team and tell them that you had to quit. I was trying to encourage you to see what you think tomorrow and not to send an email in the middle of the night.

My perspective is for situations like this, it is never good to explain over email. No one knows what's behind it, and its tone cannot be heard. It's so much better to pick up the phone. The right thing was to talk to your coach and see what he thought and could recommend.

I know you couldn't sleep and the wait was causing you to go crazy – pardon the pun. You got up very early to make the call. I felt that by talking, you would feel a peace.

Me: What about me changing my mind about where we were living? Should we go to Florida – no! yes!

Kevin: Yes, there were times when I got frustrated. One day you stated your choice and this was the fact, and then two days later you would change your mind and these were the facts. All I knew at that time was you really didn't know what to do. For me, it didn't matter where we were as long as we were together and we could get through it.

I think it came to crunch when I was going to Brazil. I was flying to Brazil for the World Cup with my soccer team Charlotte United. We were at the airport; you had been to see your psychologist that day, and you were saying, "I just can't do it, can't do it." I said, "We will not go to Florida."

You're not in a good place and you need to be somewhere where we have a support system with friends that we can reach out if we need help or anything. Moving to Florida was totally new; we didn't know people down there in the way that we knew the people from church and our friends as well that would could help us if we needed it.

Me: But we had actually visited Florida and you were making a commitment to Orlando City Youth.

Kevin: I do remember going to Orlando for tryouts. This would be an opportunity for us to connect with people. However, you didn't want to get out of the hotel. You refused to leave. All you wanted to do was listen to Joyce Meyer. As a side note, at that time, I didn't enjoy listening to Joyce, as I felt it was distorting your thinking at the time. Now four years later, I find myself saying, "Let's go listen to Joyce!"

Back to the story. You didn't want to leave the hotel; you didn't want to be around people, which was very difficult for me as you were normally the life and soul of parties and loved to be around people.

One night of tryouts, you did come along and promised you would walk around the fields. At tryouts, I was looking for you. I couldn't see you; you had stayed in the car the whole time.

Me: How were you feeling at that time?

Kevin: Well, I wasn't feeling anything. (Elaine: such a guy response). I know I was obviously worried about you, not knowing what was wrong with you. Was it just that you were stressed with work, or was it something more? But regardless, whatever it was, I had this feeling that God will put it right; God will give us the answers. I didn't want it to be me that's making the decision and then it doesn't work out because it's not God's plan, so it was a case of waiting to see how it worked out and what was going to happen.

We came back from the tryouts, that was in May. Beginning of July is when I went to Brazil and it was on the plane, and I contacted Charlotte United and told them I was not going to Florida. They were so gracious and said they would look after me. They will always

113

have work for me. When I returned from Brazil, I also has to speak to Orlando City to let them know that it wasn't possible for us to move because of Elaine's health. We needed to stay here, where we had a good support system and maybe will look at it again next year see how things go. They were very understanding as well. They told me to do what I needed to do.

Me: You spent time to encourage me to exercise every day. Why did you do that?

Kevin: It's important to have a healthy body. I wanted to help you get out for a walk. It was important to be doing something: active body creates an active mind.

Me: As time progressed, how did you feel about the fact I didn't like what you wanted me to do?.

Kevin: I was at peace. I felt the strongest both physically and mentally at this time. I would go to F3 workouts at five-thirty am. This helped me to be supported by fellow Christian guys who could support me and pray for you. I knew that when you made statements such as "God has left me," I simply reassured you He had not. I didn't preach. I know that He never leaves you or forsakes you.

Me: What about the fact that I didn't want to go to the doctor?

Kevin: You have never liked to go to the doctor. You feel that you should be able to deal with things God's way and He can fix it. However, I believe (and I know that you believe) that God uses all people and gives them the gifts and talents to help others. I know that going to see a psychiatrist and being prescribed medication is not something that was easy for you to accept.

I'm not a doctor; however, I had been speaking to others who had been in similar situations. I was convinced you had a chemical imbalance and that you needed professional help. And I was aware that if you started to take medication, it would take six to eight weeks to kick-in, which would be challenging for you, as you needed to see immediate results.

I'm glad you did take the medication. I think it's more acceptable in the United States to get treatment than it is in the UK. It seems that in the United States, many people have psychiatrists or see therapists.

It was hard to get you to see a psychiatrist. The morning that we had to go for the first visit was challenging. When you woke up, you decided that you didn't want to go because of a dream you had. It was at this point I had to use "tough love." I had to get you there, and so basically helped you dress and took you to the car. I know that entire experience at the time was not pleasant for you.

Me: What about the decision to all Orlando City and tell them you were not coming?

Kevin: Yes, it was hard for me, but easy at the same time. I knew it was the right thing to do. We had our support system in Charlotte, our church, our friends. We would not have any support in Florida. Thankfully, Orlando City was very understanding.

Me: Tell the readers about the time you wanted me to go to the Liverpool FC soccer game with you.

Kevin: Our friend had come over to ride with me to the soccer game. We were ready to get in the car and you kept switching from yes, you wanted to come with us, and now you couldn't.

I think you realized I was getting frustrated, as I wanted to go to the game, so you decided to say ok and come with us. You sat in the back of the car like a little girl, all nervous like you didn't really know where you were going.

When we got to the stadium, as we drove to find a place to park, you decided that you were not able to go through with it and decided to go home. It was really sad for me. I was worried because you were going home on your own; however, you assured me you that you would be ok.

I wanted to share this experience with you, and I thought it would be good for you to be out with people. But no, you took the car after dropping us off.

Then I receive a call from you telling me that you had changed your mind, but I had already given away your ticket. The game was not enjoyable. We also had to get the train home! Was I being selfish wanting you to be at the game with me?

Me: What about the weekend when I try to kill myself?

Kevin: Yes, we had been to church and you felt like the pastor had given a message that Jesus was the only answer and not to go waste money on a psychiatrist. You learned later that you misheard the message and this was validated by a follow-up conversation with the pastor.

After church, I had a coaching clinic at the club that I had to attend. At the end, people wanted to stop me and ask questions. I knew I was running late and I knew that you would not be happy about that. I texted you to let you know I was on my way home.

When I got home, I thought to myself *Oh my! I must have done something wrong!* You didn't look like you were in a good place. (Little did I know that you had just tried to attempt suicide!) You thought you were being all nice! We went to our neighbor to have dinner and you kept giving me dirty looks. I was wondering what I had wrong!

It wasn't till the next day that it all came to light. You told me what you had tried to do the day before, and that you were going downstairs to do it now! You really thought I was going to let you do that! You actually said, "I'm going downstairs to get the knives!" I stopped you, but I couldn't stop you from screaming.

I called two people: Christine to help me help you. Also, the psychiatrist. He told me that you need to go to the ER. Little did I know what that would mean.

Christine came over to help me get you dressed and to the car. I'm not sure where you got your strength from, because you were fighting both of us as you didn't want to get in the car. We thought we were taking you to an urgent care; what we didn't know was it was a place for suicidal people.

Me: What about the hospital experience?

Kevin: We were not in the waiting room very long, and your name was called. The experience was quite different than a regular hospital. In order to get to see the doctor, I had to remove everything from my pockets and leave them in a safety deposit box.

Then I went to see the doctor. He was trying to explain to you how the hospital is like a resort. You were not accepting anything that he said. I was concerned. He asked to speak with me and Christine separately.

I can't recall the questions he asked me. All I recall is him telling me that you will need to be committed and go to the hospital for help. That was really hard for me to hear. It was a hard thing to admit that my wife needs to go into a mental institution. However, I knew deep down that this was the only way that you would get the help you need. It was all a shock and happening so fast. The next thing I know is that they are calling for a car for you to take you to the hospital.

When you get in the car, which I remember looking like a secure police car, your face looked so scared. You just kept looking at me and making hand gestures for me to help you. It was so hard to see you in a car that had bulletproof glass section.

We arrived at the "resort" and you were taken into a secure courtyard. We saw the garage door go up and then close behind you. It was eerily quiet.

Christine and I went in to be sure you were ok. It was visiting hours. I would get used to these very quickly. It was so hard for me to think that you were in this place with these people. But I knew it was the best place for you. Don't you just hate tough love!

Christine and I would coordinate so that she would come see you first after work, and then after I had finished my soccer training, I would come by and Christine would leave. It seemed to work well.

The hardest part for me was not to be able to touch you. There was a no-contact rule. We were not able to be intimate. What I meant by that was we were not able to kiss or hug. To me, that made me feel like a prisoner, even though I respected and understood the rules.

There was a mixed bag of some quiet, and some very loud. As I spoke to the nurses and admin, one of the things they shared with me was their record of "getting people out." Their stats were that they were able to get people out within five to seven days. I shared that with you, and I am sure your performance related self-kicked in and you were determined to get out in that timeframe.

This came to light when you told me the doctors were talking to you about leaving. You told me that you were telling them whatever they needed to hear so you could "get out." Of course, I wanted you home more than anything; however, I had to tell the nurse what you told me. This meant that you were to stay at the hospital. It hurt me; however, once again tough love had to kick in. I didn't want to be responsible for you to come home too soon and then do something I would later regret.

Me: What support did you have during this time?

Kevin: I drew on the support of my friends. I was part of an early morning fitness group at that time called F3: Faith, Fitness, Fellowship. I was able to share with them what was going on in my life, and also have them pray for me. My advice to anyone who is dealing with the hurt of someone is to have a strong support system. I knew that I could call any of these guys, any time, and they would be there for me.

I also wanted to call out Chris Holmes; he was also there for me and would share what he had been learning about mental health and is always there for me.

I have to admit I felt the most peace and strength during this time. I knew in my heart of hearts that everything was going to be ok. I can understand and I have sympathy with people that are involved with family members that are going through something similar. I can say to them while I don't know all your details, I do know what it's like to go through this and although it was the worst time of my life, I did feel mentally and physically my strongest, and that's definitely down to God being with me at that time. He is always with me.

Me: Describe what it was like the day you came to pick me up and heard that I had to continue outpatient treatment.

Kevin: I actually didn't feel very comfortable about you coming out; I didn't feel like you were ready. I was thankful to hear that you still had some accountability to go to the outpatient center full time.

What hurt me the most was what you said to me that day when we got back home.

We were playing a game – Mastermind – we very rarely played games, but you saw this as a healing strategy. At the end of the game, you said: "I don't think I love you anymore. I don't think I have ever loved you!"

That felt like a punch to my stomach. I couldn't believe it; I didn't want to believe it. After all we had just been through and would continue to go through.

I took a deep breath and didn't respond. I could only pray that you didn't mean it because you were still not fully healed.

I relate to having to give your children tough love. For example, they do something wrong so you take away their privileges – say, for example, being able to drive the car. What that means for you is that now your schedule is messed up because you have to take them places. And you know that what you are doing will help them grow.

So, for me, now that you were back at home and in outpatient, it was great, even though I had to change my schedule. It was worth it.

Each day I would meet you at three pm and we would go walk the mall because it was too hot outside. I know that even to this day, you really don't like to spend too much time in the mall. Then when we returned home, you would spend time with Olga while I went to training. Between myself and Olga, we were able to support you and be there for you.

What was also good is that I was able to control you taking your medication. I would be sure that you took your pills each night. I would hide them from you, as I really didn't know where you were mentally. You told me you were fine, but that is what you said last time!

Me: When did you start to see the change in me?

Kevin: We went on the cruise (which had been booked a year previous) to see Angela. You were one person out and about on the cruise, as you mixed with people. You were not very nice to me; in fact, you were nasty. However, I knew this was not the real you.

I could see you changing a bit as you continued to mix with more people on the cruise. It was the last day that you told me you felt ready to go back to work; well what you really said is that you could go and work at Publix and talk to people. You did say that you felt like the light switch had come on.

It had been approximately six to eight weeks since you had started to take your medication consistently. I was a little leery about you going to work, as it was work that had taken you over the edge. Again, I had to trust.

Thankfully you take your pill a day and that seems to keep you balanced. I know that you want to come off the pill and you will eventually at the right time. It's all in God's timing.

It's interesting because sometimes you forget to take your pill and I can tell. I see a change in your disposition.

Me: What advice would you give to family members when they are in similar situations?

Kevin: If they know the Lord to definitely trust in Him. For you, it was a combination of the Lord and medication that worked. For me, it was the combination of the Lord and my support system.

Similar to how important it was for you to have a support system, it's the same for the main supporter to have family and /or friends to reach out to and lean on.

You need to practice "tough love." If you have kids, you already know this is super hard to do. Using tough love on your spouse/loved one is even more difficult, but so worth it.

Be there and listen. Don't preach. Speak plain and simple truth. Like you are doing writing this book; as the supporter it is also important to share your story. You really don't know who needs to hear it. Be open and be the light that you have been called to be. Don't hide in the dark with the shame.

Quite often, it is those who are going through the struggle that get the most attention and help. You as the supporter also need the same level of care and attention.

Keep yourself strong and be there for your loved one. I have heard stories where couples have split, broken relationships. I want to encourage you that if you are thinking of throwing in the towel, don't! It is one of the hardest places to be but it's all worth it when you come through the other side. Our relationship is a lot deeper; we have come to know each other more than we ever would have done.

Me: Any last words?

Kevin: I want to tell everyone how much I love you. You are the love of my life, an amazing woman, strong, well educated, powerful woman of God who is a leader and passion about what she does. You want to help others and I love you for that and thank Jesus for you. English Elaine, you are my world.

The Power of Friends

Before we hear from Christine, my prayer partner, I want to do a shout-out to all my friends that I know or did not know were there for me.

Jennifer L. was always a phone call away. However, when I got really bad, I would not let her in. At the start, I would go to her house and we would have a cup of tea and sit out on her porch. We would share stories of what was going on her life. We would encourage each other and keep pointing each other to the truth in Christ. As I got worse, I did less talking. It was great for her to still talk about her life and I was a willing listener, although I must confess I am not sure how much I heard and I was just making the appropriate nods and the right "umm," "ahh," and "yes" sounds at the right time. I have since apologized for that. She is the friend who drove to see me on the day I was taken to the resort. However, she saw Christine's car on the driveway and thought that Christine was with me and decided not to stop! If only she knew what was going on at the time with me being in the ER room.

Nate and Jen: Oh my! They are the couple that live in Atlanta that I went to stay with and ended up with a staying and having a "crazy weekend."

Julie: She was on the other side of the country. She felt like she was out of control, and my friends were not doing all that they could do! She was the one that made a call to help direct my time. She called and encouraged me (or should I say told me) to simply get off the sofa and clean my floor. It was hard but I did it because I felt account-able. She was also the person that called me when I was writing my suicide letter. I recall the phone ringing and with tears rolling down my eyes, I knew that I could not pick up the phone and tell her I was ready to kill myself.

Diana: She came to help counsel me through the days at the start. She predicted that I would end up in a psych unit and that I would hear people screaming! Maybe she has the gift of prophesy.

I'm sure there are other friends that were praying for me. I thank each one of you. Know that each person impacted me and your prayers were answered.

Finally, my friend Christine, my prayer partner. The one friend that I let in, I wanted to give her the opportunity to share what the crazy summer was like from her perspective.

A Friend's Perspective:

Originally when Elaine and I talked about my writing a chapter for her book, I was thinking I might be the comic relief, as there were many moments that at the time were not funny to me (well maybe a little), but NOW... you just have to laugh!! As I sit down to write though, I'm not confident I can convey the humor of them well, and I'm unsure what exactly to write but anyway...here goes!!!

As just stated, I'm a bit unclear what to share... I was there for a lot of Elaine's journey and found it difficult to know how to best support her. We probably should, but have never had a conversation about her opinions regarding what kind of support was helpful to her, and what was not. I find people have to work through some things for themselves (meaning you cannot do it for them; there is no combination of just the right words that will make them see the light) but you CAN give support through time, prayer, fasting, and encouragement, even if it seems to fall on deaf ears. You never know what is getting through.

From day one, when she decided to quit her job, Elaine could articulate truth, but she was struggling (and failing) to live out of it. She and I had been prayer partners for many, many years – meeting at Starbucks once a week, and then weekly and sometimes daily morning calls when she was travelling to catch up and pray. We were also both counselors at a ministry that "teaches the gospel to Christians." Here we taught others how to recognize the lies they were believing and living from, and to choose to believe the truth about themselves and their identity in Christ. She knew she was not a failure; that she could do all things through Christ who strengthens her; that she didn't have to be perfect; and that she was loved, valued, and accepted, even if she made mistakes.

I also knew that my speaking truth to her could be helpful, but was not the life-breathing, life-changing, wound-healing encounter she truly needed, which was listening to her "Papa," Father God, whispering these truths to her. I did speak truth; I tried to encourage. I tried to listen and "be there" for her, but also not let her get on the fear and worry train for long. I prayed… I spent time with her.

We did a lot of walking our dogs at Squirrel Lake Park, we hiked Crowder's Mountain, she went to holy yoga with me, we got coffee at Starbucks like the old days (well, but not really like the old days, if ya know what I mean). I know she spent a significant amount of time (hours and hours) on her own, trying to engage God for healing (journaling, praying, shouting at the devil).

I could see how an absolute "perfect storm" of events and challenges collided, causing Elaine her "summer from #!@&!!." She was put forward as the best her company had to offer at a specific type of work for a big, household name company, and then placed under a manager who didn't follow her recommendations, didn't give her support, and gave her the message satisfying the client was ALL up to her (I'd be stressed too!!).

One of the other pieces was that her green card was coming up for renewal and she was very worried if she was not working OR she had a mental diagnosis, she would be denied. Add to THAT, she was the primary breadwinner and they were talking about moving to Florida – need I remind you that moving is one of the higher stressful life events we go through? I can't remember if Kevin had quit his job yet or was still working but, whew, I can feel my blood pressure rising just thinking about all that again!!

That first day, when she called to say she quit her job, I was kind of surprised, confused, and to be honest, a little hurt too. I am an introvert (she always teased me about leaving her parties early, like ten pm – YEP!! I'm tired and overstimulated!! I really don't think extroverts understand us introverts). Anyway, she is the OPPOSITE. Maybe she has insecurities, but she is not afraid to speak her mind, has never met a stranger (yes, one of her gifts is evangelism - and she even had a "stranger prayers" blog at one point where she offered to pray for a stranger every day), and she liked to constantly challenge herself.

I'm so glad SHE approached ME about being prayer partners so many years earlier. I knew when she started doing consulting work there were days she really dreaded work, even got sick to her stomach, but then she would push through and shine. In hindsight, this may have been an early indicator of her struggle but she hadn't talked about this that much lately. Since she had started traveling almost a hundred percent of the time, we were not as consistent about praying together, but why had she not reached out for prayer earlier? I do think we had been praying about it, but I don't remember understanding how close to the edge she was. Why was I so surprised by her announcement from the couch saying she QUIT her job, which meant she declined the offer to work a few more days and be rolled off the project, and she declined taking a short leave; she… just…. quit? (Thank goodness for a great team and manager who didn't accept her resignation and gave her the leave option anyway!!). Who was this person before me? Why was I not aware how much she was struggling? (Side note: Some days I didn't want to be honest with what was really bothering me.)

We all have different issues we struggle with. There were days I didn't want to say, "Yep, can you pray for THAT... AGAIN..." It felt like admitting I was losing the battle with a certain issue that day meant I was a failure, and not living in the victory I know is mine. It seemed easier not to be reminded of my defeat by asking for prayer… and I was afraid Elaine might think "Really? Again? That?" Such a good plan of the enemy to keep me isolated and uncovered in prayer don't ya think?

I'm not saying this is what Elaine was doing... I'm just saying I tend to do that... AND... It made me sad I didn't realize how much she was struggling. And ... WHY did she not take one of the offers they gave her to not give up totally?!! They were willing to work with her!!

So, I could see why she was struggling with the thoughts she was having...but how, Lord, do you want me to help her? From her first days after stepping back from work while she was fixating on certain lies (I can't do it, I'll never work again, I'm going to lose my green card....etc.), she could articulate the truth...she was just not living in it or believing it, and I struggled to know how best to help her during this time.

We were counselors at a Christian ministry and we both knew that engaging God in the middle of her mess was the answer, and I KNOW she tried. We took walks and talked, she spent countless hours at local parks journaling and reading Scripture, praying (I assume), and reaching out to receive what she needed from Papa God, but it didn't seem to be helping. Again, she could articulate truth, but at the moment it seemed to be head knowledge only and not invading her life in any way.

I'm a strong advocate of giving advice only when it's asked for or when God specifically tells you to, and otherwise, be quiet!! Early on, while I tried not to say it or give advice, my opinion would have been that she shouldn't try medicine...that she should try counseling and engaging God for her healing (which she was doing).

As time went by though, I did start to wonder if medicine was going to be part of the answer. Her doctors had started recommending med- icine but she wanted no part of that! "Americans take too many pills." It seemed like everyone was giving her advice - "Take the medicine" or "Don't take the medicine - trust God," "Have faith, don't you have enough faith?" Grrrrrr, I didn't have a clear idea what God wanted so I kept my mouth shut and was a bit ticked at how easily others KNEW what she NEEDED to do. I'd be confused too!!

Of course, even with all their advice, she was hearing what she wanted... one Sunday, our pastor was trying to say people go to pills too quickly... some people who struggle with depression instead of first running to pills might try spending time with God and counseling. He was emphasizing how quick we are to turn to medicine when sometimes the issues are spiritual, not physical. What did Elaine hear? She shouldn't take pills (even though by this time all her doctors were recommending them, and I completely agreed it was time).

At some point, I picked the "Hope in Front of Me" song by Danny Gokey as "Elaine's song" (meaning my song for her). Hopelessness seems to go hand in hand with depression. Elaine had lost hope and no one could help her find it. I can't say I myself ever lost hope for her, but there sure were days where I wondered where this was going. I knew God could heal her instantly if He chose to. God was a good God, and was for her. Despite this, at times I did wonder what the future held. If she continued this downward spiral, she might lose her job, they might lose their house, Kevin might have to take a different job to support them. They may lose their green card status and have to move back to England. I did, however, have HIGH confidence Elaine was NOT going to end up a destitute, crazy, homeless person on the street, which was what she was envisioning.

It was after she had gone to Atlanta to visit a friend that I became convinced it was time for medicine. Apparently while there, she was walking around the house yelling at Satan, which her friends found very disturbing. I saw her on her drive home and she looked disheveled, even shaking a bit; she had a look in her eye like a scared animal. I felt it was time for medicine and started encouraging her to consider it, but did not tell her this was what she "should" do (pet peeve of mine, can you tell?) not that it mattered — no one was going to convince her!! I realized then that she may have to deteriorate to a point where someone else would "force" her to take medication.

I still remember walking around the mall that day on her way home from Atlanta. We replayed the same conversation every time we got together and I'm sure we were both tired of it. I think it was this trip I was talking about head knowledge versus heart knowledge and she "hadn't appropriated it yet" and … did she remember THAT comment and will NEVER let me live that down!! (Ha!!). I said ALOT of things over those months (and I might add that there were a lot of things I was able to hold my tongue about and NOT say!) but this comment stuck and in a BAD way. It must have made her feel judged, or frustrated, or something! Yes, "appropriated" is a big word, but I was talking about the disconnect between her head knowledge and heart/actions using language we were both familiar with from Grace Life.

How do I know this stuck with her? Months later, after she was "back to herself," she liked to sarcastically sneer, "I know you 'know' it but have you 'appropriated' it yet?" and I would think to myself, *Out of all the stuff I said, that's the thing that got through and you remember? jeeesh!!*

I just wanted to comment here how isolating struggling with a mental illness is. Elaine didn't want to tell everyone her story or explain what was going on, so her circle became smaller and smaller. This also meant that she was going out less because she didn't want to run into people she knew. This is an overlooked fact with mental illness. At a time when she needed the most support and prayer, she was the also the most isolated. One close friend who I thought knew everything as Elaine was spending a lot of time at her house it turns out knew almost nothing! Elaine spent the time listening to this friend share about her own struggles - and she truly was going through something huge herself. I don't mean to make light of that.

I wrestled with what to say when people asked about her. Many seemed to know a bit of her situation, but not the full story. I finally just decided to say, "She could use your prayer" and for anything further would direct them to call her or Kevin, as I did not want to give out more information than they wanted me to.

And another side note: one of our friends had moved back to California recently and was struggling with being so far away. She was seeing the changes in Elaine and wanting to DO something. She would call Elaine and try to help her by helping her come up with plans for the day: "What does Kevin want you to do? Clean? Okay let's make a list …what's the first thing you need to do?" When she realized Elaine had zero processing ability or problem-solving skills at the moment, and couldn't manage to get one thing on her list done — or maybe she couldn't even write the list — she would call us (friends) freaking out. I got the impression she felt we were not doing enough, or caring for Elaine well. If she were still in Charlotte, I think she would have force-fed Elaine pills at some point, or done an "involuntary commitment" ahead of our timing. Ultimately, I think she (like the rest of us) just wanted to help but felt powerless to do so. But, again, short of involuntary commitment (and maybe we waited too long, I don't know) I'm not sure what else we could have done. Elaine was DETERMINED not to take pills and no logic or reasoning was getting through.

And then it happened…

The worst day of my life: I find this funny now, but it wasn't then. Six am, I'm doing a morning devotional and taking time to ask God, "What do You have to say to me today?" I don't often hear something concrete but on this day, I CLEARLY hear "Go to Elaine's." Since Elaine was "so much fun" (Yes, I'm being sarcastic) to be with at this time, I answered back, "Do I have to go over there? Can't I just call...?" and IMMEDIATELY my cell phone rings. It says it is Elaine. I answered and it's Kevin (her husband) saying, "Christine can you come over?" I hear Elaine in the background screaming at the top of her lungs "Noooooo...". I think to myself, *Okay God, got it!*

I guess she had taken some pills the night before, but then heard Kevin coming home so spit them out, but did tell him. It was a defining moment. She was no longer safe to be left alone. The challenge of the day was to commit Elaine to inpatient treatment (which meant she would have a diagnosis that could hinder her green card renewal) and somehow talk her into agreeing so it would not be listed as "involuntary" (cannot remember why that was important at the moment – probably also had to do with her green card.).

It was heartbreaking to see her. She had lost so much weight; she looked like a skeleton. Her clothes hung on her. She was shaking a bit and had that scared animal look in her eyes. She didn't fiercely resist, but there was a lot of talking about needing to go see a doctor, coaxing, and yes, a little bit of carrying/dragging to get her in the vehicle. Kevin discreetly packed some clothes in the car so she didn't see it. She seemed to buy into the idea that we were just "going to see the doctor."

I found it funny (now, not then, of course) how unaware of her situation (meaning OUT OF IT) she was. We ended up (Kevin, Elaine, and myself) sitting in a small room for hours at the clinic in between interviews and such. She was acting <u>exactly</u> like I would expect a "crazy person" to act. She looked wide-eyed and anxious, her hair was disheveled and a bit greasy, and she would rock back and forth in her chair.

She kept twirling her hair with her finger. She kept rolling up the scrubs they gave her to hide the part that had the name of the hospital, and she spent time tearing a piece of paper into smaller and smaller pieces. At one point (I found this to be welcomed comic relief) she was standing in the hall, waiting for the security guard to unlock the bathroom for her. She was looking at me and nodding her head behind her at the people wandering the halls, which I interpreted to mean "Oh my gosh!! Look at all the crazy people here," and I had to try REALLY HARD to stifle a laugh, thinking, *Oh my gosh, if you could just see your reflection right now...girl YOU TOTALLY FIT in here. You look JUST like them...!!* Sigh...maybe you had to be there, but I found it VERY funny. I could still roll around laughing thinking about it.

We FINALLY got her to sign the papers voluntarily (yay...). I'll never forget the moment they led her away to drive up to the inpatient facility (we couldn't drive with them). She was looking back at us with a scared look, but also a look that seemed to say, "What have you done to me? How can you leave me here?" I couldn't help but cry and turn away. I didn't want to make her more afraid. I felt like a bad friend...would she ever forgive me? I knew we were doing the right thing, but it felt like we were betraying her. Kevin and I drove behind them up to the inpatient facility. During the drive, Elaine was looking out the back window at us, scared, with that, "What have you done to me?" look. I tried to remind myself that we were helping her and this was for her good.

About half an hour later, after her arrival, it was visiting time and we sat at a table with her — now wrapped in a blanket but still rocking with that crazy, scared look in her eye. She looked around at all the other clients. I can no longer remember her exact words, but she said something like, "You can't leave me here; these people look crazy" and

I think this time we did tell her, "Sorry to tell you this, Elaine, but you fit right in here!! You look just like them!!"

This is a funny NOW but not really then…and sorry ya just had to be there.

First visiting hours Kevin and I both attended, they only gave you an hour and a half. We both went in about the same time. Elaine started telling Kevin, "There's something I have to tell you; I have to confess…you're never going to forgive me." Kevin was being very sweet and he told her "you don't have to tell me…whatever it is I forgive you." I correctly guessed she was thinking about confessing about a time of unfaithfulness early in their marriage before they knew Jesus and I'm thinking to myself, *Noooooo… Please don't tell him that… you need all the support you can get right now and that's one of those things that makes men walk away…you REALLY cannot afford to hurt him any more at this time when he is exhausted and trying hard to be there for you.*

So, I told her…. "See? Kevin says he already forgives you…you really don't have to tell him." Elaine, with a tortured look on her face, kept going back to "No…I really need to tell you this Kevin." We went in circles like this for like forty-five minutes. I wanted to stay to prevent her from telling him, but I felt they should also have time alone so I left after forty-five minutes but waited outside. So, what happened? Did she tell him? Somehow that doesn't seem like that's mine to share!

So, the whole time Elaine was in inpatient rehab, she was saying, "I could run these classes, I just tell them what they want to hear so I can get out of here but, I'm still going to kill myself." My thoughts were: *Doesn't anyone see through her? God, I have faith You can heal and help her but, she's in here now and not getting better. How is this going to end?* She did get out fairly quickly and transitioned to a day program (I think she's calling this the spa). A few of us took turns having dinner with her when Kevin had soccer so she wasn't alone, as she was STILL saying she cannot go back to work and she was going to kill herself. (ARGH!!) What do you do with someone like that? I kept spending time with her and praying.

Soon I heard a testimony at church from missionaries who are working with Native Americans about some truly miraculous physical healings, and also about a significant drop in the suicide rate on their reservation after intentional prayer and fasting. The verse, "This kind cannot come out except by prayer and fasting", (Mark 9:29) came to mind. I felt the Lord was telling me something here, but I wasn't completely sure so I debated it; but ultimately decided it could not hurt so why not err on the side of obedience if I even "think" this (fasting) might be something He is calling me to?

I decided to commit to fasting on Wednesdays for a month. A few other of our mutual friends agree to pray and fast with me, and we set up times to call each other to pray on fasting days. There were maybe five of us fasting? My husband even decided to join us, which I thought was so sweet!! Anyone who could, would call at a certain time and pray for Elaine with a particular emphasis on suicide.

It was a slow, gradual transition, but week 1 she was still strongly stating she was going to kill herself and it felt like by week 2, her resolve was weakening a little. Week 3 she was preparing to go on a cruise but when she got back... you guessed it – she was going to kill herself. She still "couldn't work" and was going to lose her green card and be homeless (aren't you tired of hearing it here in my story too?!!). She was stating this in a very matter of fact way. (Again, as a friend hearing this for the literally 698th time, how do you lovingly and encouragingly respond to that? I think I started trying to make a joke out of it, "Well I hope I get your piano." Probably not the right response.)

Anyway, week 4: sometime towards the end of her cruise, she decided she could see herself going back to work. When she returned from the cruise, she was like a whole new person!! She suddenly had a shift in her thinking/beliefs and had no difficulty picturing herself going back to work!! Whoa.

Later, when I am spending time with the Lord, I asked Him what shifted Elaine. Was it that the medicine had time to kick in, or was it the prayer and fasting, or both? I smiled as I heard Him say, "Just give Me glory," which I understand to mean "I'm not answering that because you will be tempted to want to take credit, or turn the fasting into a 'key to unlocking the…blah blah blah' rather than just following my lead. And if I tell you the medicine you will think your fasting was a waste of time. Just know I am the healer (no matter how I choose to do it), be thankful Elaine has been restored, and…give Me glory!!"

So… my takeaways from this whole experience:

1) Don't be afraid to ask for prayer …for anything, for the same thing over and over if you have to… Cherish people willing to pray with you and for you.

2) Realize people are going through things that they aren't sharing… don't assume people are fine.

3) Often people with mental health issues are afraid to share and it makes them isolated… don't back off; be consistent and hang in there with them.

4) Thank you, God, for the gift of medication, AND thank you God for Your healing!

PART 4 – Life Now

What is life like now?

This next section is intended to continue to give you hope. There is life on the other side of the deepest, darkest place where you have been.

As the proverbial saying goes, "Light at the end of the tunnel."

Five Years Later

Today, I'm on a plane flying to a client site. Yes, I am back in consulting. Each day I am very thankful for where I am. I am able to meet lots of different people at the airport – going to and from the client site. And I meet lots of people in the city that I am working.

Yes, my goal is to make an impact on my team and with the client; however, my broader goal is to bring light and joy; to help people experience what that looks like. I have received lots of positive feedback from my clients and teams that I bring joy and light to the teams. I am so thankful for that. Praise God – thank you.

I recently received a message through my Instagram account @therealenglishelaine from a former client and she shared the image below.

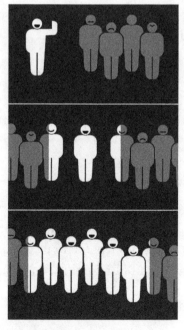

She told me I was the white person, the light, and how I have left a legacy. This is so humbling and also so inspiring. My desire is to continue to be the light that I have been called to be.

Where am I living now? We made it to Central Florida. That was a God story.

After my crazy summer, my husband was able to commit to working for Orlando City Youth organization. Thank you to them that they had the patience to wait for him. In my eyes, he's the best soccer coach.

The story behind where we ended up in Central Florida looks like this. We had no idea where to live. Our deciding factor was based on my husband's job. Remember, I travel each week, so as long as I am not too far from the airport, I am happy to live wherever. One of our key criteria was to be on the north of the I-4, simply because south of the I-4 is where all the international tourists come to stay for Disney. So north of I-4 it is. As we began to look at the neighborhoods, it was quite over our price range, if we were to live close to the soccer complex.

My question to Kevin:

"How far in travel time are you prepared to be from work?"

Reply: "No more than one hour."

We drew an arc of travel one hour north of the I-4. We spent a lot of time online looking. We decided on a few properties and contacted Kevin's friend, who is a realtor in Central Florida. The story behind the friend is that he is an old school friend from Kevin's childhood. How crazy is that connection?

He would look at the properties and make an assessment for us. Easter weekend we decided to make a trip. We really didn't want to pay for a hotel. In a conversation with a leader that I had connected with, the same leader who referred me into the new role that I took when I came back to work from my crazy summer, I mentioned I was going to Mount Dora. She smiled and shared she had a vacation rental and she would be happy for us to stay. Thank you, Jesus.

Good Friday, we drive to Florida with our dog to look at a piece of land, as we thought we could build as an option. The land was not viable, so we decide to go into Mount Dora and make our plans for the rest of the weekend.

Mount Dora is such a quaint place. It reminded us of the Lake District in England; it even had an English pub. We found a little coffee / donut shop. Kevin and our realtor friend went inside to place the order. I stayed outside with the dog.

A lady walked out of the coffee shop and struck up a conversation. Dogs are good conversation-starters. She was curious about why we were in the area. I shared that we were looking for a property.

"Oh, that's great," she replied. "My mum is selling her house."

I reply, "Where?"

"Eustis."

"Oh, that's far away from here."

She replied: "No, it's less than ten minutes from here."

"Does it have a swimming pool?"

"No, it's on a lake."

"Hmm, that is a non-negotiable for us."

She tells us the price, over our budget.

She hands me her card. Yup, she is a realtor and selling her mum's house!

Kevin and our realtor friend came out of the coffee shop and made introductions.

We continued on with our day and were very thankful to my colleague for allowing us to stay at her home.

Easter Sunday. We decided to go visit Real Life Christian Church, Mount Dora Campus. We had been looking online for a church. Our Google search was "non-denominational, Christian, grace." Real Life was top of the list.

It looked like a small campus, compared to our current church. The internet told us there was one service at ten am.

Easter Sunday, we arrived at the church at 9:45 am. Because it was Easter, there were two services: nine am and eleven am! We were either too late or way too early.

We decided to go and look at the property that the lady at the coffee shop told us about. "Let's just go and see how far away it is from the church."

We drove no more than fifteen minutes. The drive took us through one of the most scenic routes through East Crooked Lake Drive. It was breathtaking. We turned into our road and saw the house. "Not too bad – but it's all battleship gray. Hmm. Not what we were expecting."

We drove past the house and looked down the driveway. Oh my! The view was the most amazing! It was glorious. We loved it. We made an appointment to look inside.

Easter Sunday service was incredible. We loved the church: so welcoming and friendly, and very Bible-based. We felt at home on day 1.

Easter Monday, we went to visit several houses. The last one of the days was the house from the lady in the coffee shop. We entered the front door, and the realtor stood there. The room was simple, not very inspiring. The staircase was very traditional. Loved it.

The conversation went something like this:

Me: "Well, that was a God meeting on Saturday!"

"Yes, are you believers?"

"Yes."

She smiled and replied, "I've been praying for this home to go to a believer. My dad recently passed. He was a pastor and the house is now too big for my mum. They have lived here for the last thirty years."

She took us through the front room to the kitchen. The kitchen was pink! Hmmm. This will need a lot of work. However, I looked straight ahead. There was a window that must have been about 10x6 ft. It looked onto the lake. It was a million-dollar view. The house was nowhere near that price. We loved it. The view was priceless. I had forgotten about the "need" for a swimming pool.

We wandered around the house. Each room that was facing the lake had picture windows and doors. The entire house was painted gray and it had a pink kitchen! All I saw is the lake, a real fireplace, a great staircase: everything that I could have imagined. Let's do it. Let's work the numbers.

The next day, Tuesday evening, we were sitting in the English pub and signing the contract for the house. We moved in a month later and four years later, still enjoy going to Real Life Christian Church in Mount Dora. The church members are our family. It has grown from one service to one service on Saturdays and two services on Sundays.

I continued to serve using my story. One year, I was a co-facilitator for the Real Freedom program. I was able to use my crazy summer experience to help others find freedom. I am also a care counsellor and connect with women who are looking for help. I am so thankful that I am able to take the time to do this. Thank you, Jesus.

I still take my medication daily; one day I will work with my doctor to come off them. What I really appreciate now is that when bad stuff happens, which it will, I am able to take a pause, recognize what is happening, take some deep breaths, and realize that I no longer need to focus on those thoughts. As the Lord says in His word: "Submit to the Lord. Resist Satan and he will flee" (James 4:7). I change my mindset; I don't ruminate. Joyce Meyer will say in her book "Battlefield of the Mind" that the battle is truly in the mind (Meyer 2017). I fully subscribe to this.

We are called to "renew our mind daily" (Rom. 12:2). I have found that sometimes I have to renew my mind hourly, and even minute by minute. I often take deep breaths. I do look at each person differently. When I see someone who is stressed, who doesn't want to listen, wants to be in control, rather than "fearing" them, or thinking bad about them, I remind myself that I have no idea what's going on in this person's life that is driving these behaviors; or even that some people have deep-rooted issues that haven't been healed and show up in all different ways. My prayer is if that is you and you are reading this, please go and explore what resources are available to get you healing and help. My recommendation is a Christian counsellor; now you may not be in that place, and that's ok. I pray that you get the help you need in the way you need it.

I am no longer daily asking the Lord to bring a stranger to pray for. I do daily ask the Lord to use me, so that I can be His vessel in whatever way that may look like. I still make connections. Stranger prayers and connections may come in my next book. Watch this space.

The End? Not Really

This memoir truly is part of my journey. I continue to be "under construction" and won't be completed until I am in heaven. In the meantime, I want to be able to continue to be light and use my story.

In the meantime, I look up and smile that it's not lost on me that there are two topics that are connected:

My book title is "My crazy summer," and the tag line for my church is "God's crazy about you," changed lives, change lives. I am a changed life that is being used to change lives and give God all the praise for that.

I am all about being real. My church is called Real Life and my Instagram name is @therealenglishelaine.

My desire is that you have been touched by my story. If you know someone who is in the dark place, this may be used as a resource to give them hope. If that's you, in the dark place, I don't know all your details; however, I do know what it's like to be in the deepest, darkest place where I felt that the only way out was to end it all. By the grace of God (I would say), I got the help that I needed to give me the strength to be light that I am called to be. You too have your story that you can use to encourage others when you are ready. Seek the medical help you need.

If you are a supporter of someone who is in the deepest, darkest place, may this book be an encouragement to you. On the days that you feel frustrated and feel like walking out and giving up on your loved ones, don't do it. Stay where you are. Just by being there is enough, believe me. It means the world to your loved one – even though it may not seem that way.

If you got to the end of this book and would like to share your story and encouragement, please do so. Send a message on my Instagram @therealenglishelaine or to my Facebook – the real English Elaine.

You are the most important person in your life and you can make a difference.

Remember God is crazy about you.

PART 4a

It's now November 2019. I'm reviewing my book to send to the publisher. Remember I told you that my story is a journey… just like yours by the way.

Today I'm sitting in London, taking a well-deserved break. Before I left for my "sabbatical," my employment contract changed with my company. Now in the past I would be super anxious; however, I am super excited to see what the future holds. Instead of seeing a closed door that I can't walk through, this time I see a door open wide, much wider than the doors would normally allow, and although I can't see the details, I know deep down in my heart and soul that 2020 is going to be phenomenal.

Earlier this year, I established English Elaine LLC to secure the name for use in the future, as I plan to graduate as a certified human potential coach and not long after that to become a certified coach through the International Coach Federation (ICF). Watch this space. Follow me on Instagram @therealenglishelaine. #treemha #stigmafree #mentalhealth and Facebook the Real English Elaine

Last updates. I graduated. I am now officially a Certified Human Potential Coach, and working back for PwC. It's March 2020. The year has most definitely started off in a phenomenal way! Who would have thought the whole world would go on pause because of a pandemic? COVID-19, known as the Coronavirus, is here. Millions of cases have been identified and hundreds of thousands of people dead! It can be a scary time. I'm praying for wisdom and guidance for all the world leaders. Praying that if people don't already know Jesus, they come to know Him, and experience His peace. Lastly, I pray for you the reader. I pray that if this is causing you more anxiety, that you reach out people you love. It's hard in these days of isolation. I encourage you to use the technology you have available to you. Talk to someone. There are many helplines and support groups available. Check out NAMI.org. Also, National Suicide Prevention Lifeline 1-800-273-8255.

If you support someone with anxiety, pay extra attention to them, reach out more than normal. Remember my story, a simple text or call can be the difference between life and death.

Maybe, by the time you read this book, a vaccine has been found and we are in our "new normal", whatever that means or looks like.

I know that through this all God is in control and His will, will be done.

PART 5 Journal Entries

I debated whether I should share the following pages. Then I was reminded about being vulnerable. Thank you, Brené Brown, for inspiring me on this topic. If you have not listened to Brené Brown's Ted Talk on vulnerability, I would highly encourage you to do so (Brown 2010).

By reading this book, my prayer is that you understand more people than you can imagine are suffering with mental issues silently. If you notice a change in a friend or family member, reach out to them. Be there for them. There is power in community.

Mental health issues are less of a taboo than previously thought. However, I think there is some stigma out there. Thankfully many famous people have "come out" and shared their stories. For me, hearing Prince Harry share his struggles is important and inspiring. However, I will remind you of what I stated at the end of sharing my testimony at Steele Creek Church of Charlotte, when someone came and said, "Wow, it seemed like you had it all put together, I can't believe this happened to you."

Remember I am only human, you are only human, we are all only human, and we live in a broken world, which means we are vulnerable. None of us is "above it."

In true terms of vulnerability, what comes next are the pages of my journaling through my crazy summer. I decided to keep the pages in their true form and not to type them up. The reason being that on the pages, my writing style changes.

If you are going through your crazy season, you may resonate with the pages. If you are supporting someone who is going through his/her crazy season, you may at least get a glimpse into their world, knowing that what's most important is for you to simply be there for them.

If you are reading this and have come out of your crazy season, it may be a reminder for you to give thanks that you have come out of the season; that you no longer need to live in shame and darkness; that you too can be used as light and for His glory.

1. Thess. 4:13.
We all need hope.

4/10/13

1 Cor. 15.

Death is a guarantee unless Jesus
comes beforehand.

1 Moment of death spirit goes to
Christ.
Body dies - who we really are
is transported to Christ.

Those who die in Christ cease from
their labors is this well.

Those who die without Christ there
is no hope - no second chances.

Jesus conquered the grave.

Snatched up because I am his
prize possession.

Salvation is real and God is real.

9/2014.

Keep hearing the message —
I need to step out of the
boat — what is my boat?
Comfort of my job — pressure
of having to perform, pressure
of being (perfect.) → confirmed by
                        counsellor 6/11/14.

Dear Lord,
What is it that you have
for me ??
  Elaine I want you to trust
me, LEAN NOT ON YOUR
OWN UNDERSTANDING —
Acknowledge me in all your
  ways and I will direct
your paths.

Lord you are amazing and I
love you so much what do you
have in store for me?
  Elaine trust me — take
one day at a time, one step
at a time and I will direct
you.
    It would not be the end
of the world, I have my
family & my health. And

most of all I love You Jesus.
You are the most important thing
to me — am I really Elanie?
YES!!!!!

In God I trust, I will not be afraid
What can man do to me?

God you are my God and I will
always trust you.
Well Lord, you brought me
to the bottom of the valley —
nowhere to go deeper except
to look up to you — to
take your hand and be guided
by you.
Lord, I want to feel your peace
again, the peace that surpasses
all understanding

Elanie you have to _let go of_
control. You have to
trust in me if you want
that peace. Know Elanie
that I will never leave you
or forsake you. When all is
hopeless gone and it seems
like everything is lost. I am here

Lord I ask you to direct my
paths.
    Lord I ask you take my hand
and guide me to a joyful
peaceful life
    I know you don't want me to
live miserably for the next
however many years you have
for me.
Lord I praise you in the storm.
You are amazing how many
times have I said how you
are in the detail!!
    I trust you Lord to be in the
detail of my life.
    I don't ever need to be thinking
about next week. I need to
focus on you today. I need
to learn to live in the moment
and experience your presence.
    I have two today — I
gave you Dr McGrath. She is
here for you. You are not
depressed or crazy Elaine —
but you did have a panic
attack. Need to be seen
Dr McGrath has thrown you

records.

Focus on me Lord and stop trying to control + manipulate your path time to rest. This is difficult you to do train but rest and listen wait for me to direct your paths. I will guide you — you simply have to trust me. That means trusting me in, through and with everything. Remember what happened to Israelites → they roamed the desert 40 years in circles and never actually saw their final destination.

Same — do not be wise in your own eyes. Learn of your own understanding.

Lord you are my refuge and my strength.

Be thankful — you struggle with the high pressure a

Client service — you need to
tell the truth and live
with the consequences of
this decision — whether it
means you go into Ltd / 7??
or it means you leave the
firm.
Elaine ~~you cannot~~ live
this miserable life.
Your joy is in me and not
work. You have to be
honest and open your
heart. You will feel a huge
weight lifted off your
shoulders.
Work hard — work as Jude 2.
Take this time for you —
take a year. Enjoy just resting
and spending this time
with me.
Elaine ~~stopping and doing~~
~~to~~ (be perfect). Just all ok.
rest and be with me.
Yes I know it is scary
and you are trembling with
fear. But all good. I
am here for you ☺

False Evidence Appearing Real.
  Anygdala hijack!!
Take time to rest Gave
from the trauma of your
decision. It is tough decision,
but not a life threatening
decision.
Gave because I have you -
you will recove, there is
so much waiting on the
other side.

Mendo? Lord what??
You are not even going to
think about it Gave -
take this week. Take this
it is the day. This is the
day that I have made for you.
You will rejoice and be
glad in it.

Dr Menmen - So what was
Friday?? An extreme
panic attack?? need to know
for my records.

So Brent was the wrong decision -
it's past → now time to move
on and have forward.

This is a new day — the
beginning of a new life
I feel the wind blow away
the past load and bathe me
in the warmth of the sun
as I enter with faith into
what the future holds.

It will be incredible and
nothing like I could ever
imagined It really won't
be all about the money —
It will be about the impact
the joy and the peace.

The not waking up with
my head in the toilet —
or keeping Kevin awake
at night.

Lord let me practice and
speak my faith such that
     I do not fear —
I trust You Lord to take
me through the next steps
whatever they may be.

7 am to have boldness   1 Jn 2:28.

Travie don't be deceitful
be TRUTHFUL
Be authentic
Tell people from your
heart what you have
done!
They will listen, might
not understand but will
be sympathetic to you.

They want what is best
for you.

The want you to be well.

Go home — expenses —
Need sick policy.
Contact Dr Mortimer
re Fridays event and
for the next 2 weeks.

The Lord is my helper;
I will not be afraid.
What can man do to me?

Faith requires a response an
action.

Let you yes be Ye
and your No be no.

From now on
accept it, enjoy it,
Don't make
anxious

5/20
Dear Lord please give me
permission to have
restraints.
Dear Lord I know you love
me and You will and
are seeing me through this.
Why has my world come
crashing down?
It has not Elaine —
you have people who love
you, support you, care
for you. I want you to
get healthy.
To get healthy I have

to be seen.

Have you are ~~emotionally~~ exhausted ~~and~~

Dr McGovern is right you desire are suffering from a trauma & what you think may be a career limiting decision. It is not, and if it is - It is NOT the end of the world. → You CANNOT ~~control this~~ have you cannot live in this misery any longer.

~~Why~~ did What caused me to make the decision → ~~More~~ from TOO early. Pride thinking I was better than the ~~women~~ - if an actor loves what one does doesn't one act The rest of her life, if a lawyer loves what he does doesn't he practice the rest of his life. So why give away what I loved? → - thinking scheming - looking for the

next and bigger thing.
So here we are on Tuesday
May 20th 2014.
Sh trau Elaine what
you need to communicate

Why do I want to live in
chaos? I don't.

Why put myself there?
how I have totally screwed
up!!!

> Do you want to
> continue to live in
> misery – NO!!

Friday,
I am such Elaine –
because a anxiety
accentuated by external
pressures.
– Take time to rest +
relax → Biggest area of
pressure at the moment is
my job and the impact of this
on the rest of my life decisions

The pressure of the clients.

Lord what do I say / do?

Gonna be honest with
your coach & the —

Anxiety is in ② areas
① The transition about
moving back to
client service

and ② The transition
of moving to Orlando.

Moving back client service
more challenging than
I ever expected.
The reasons why I left
the TODA's faculty
member are the reasons
why I am challenged —
the pace of work, the
high pressure environment

client service — pace, pressure
less structured.

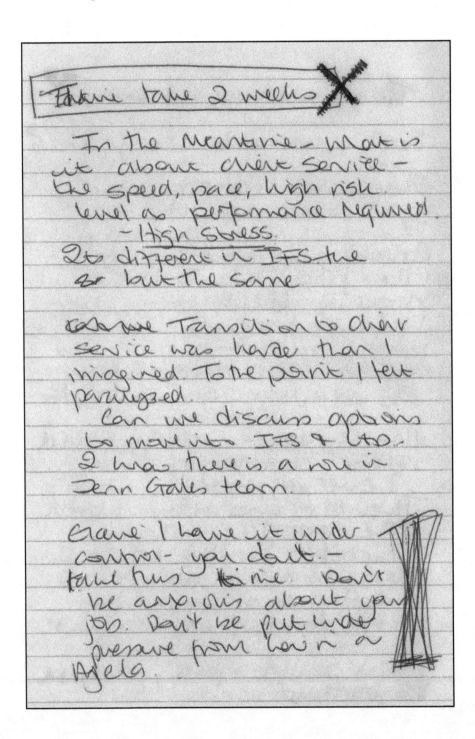

Elaine take 2 weeks ✕

In the Meantime - what is
it about client service -
the speed, pace, high risk.
level as performance required.
- High stress.
2 to different in IFS the
so but the same

Transition to client
service was harder than I
imagined. To the point I felt
paralyzed.
    Can we discuss options
to move into IFS & GTO.
2 was there is a role in
Jenn Grates team.

Elaine I have it under
control - you don't. -
take this time. Don't
be anxious about your
job. Don't be put under
pressure from Lou n or
Angela.

Have you sent the email
to Lisa — Know that I
have wrapped in my
arms.
2 Know you want to
know about your job.
Thats perfectly acceptable.
So what if you ask
earlie? — You will
know — in 2 weeks enjoy them
dont be worried by them
Have I am at a great
work and I don't want to
you to take control and
fix like you have been.

Take a deep breathe — dont
worry I have it.
It is going to be ok — may not
be like you expect —
even better!!

B. 56. 3 — 5
Whenever I am afraid
I will trust in You.
In God I have put my trust.
I will not fear.
what can flesh do to me??

Do not be afraid of man!

Elaine - fit for more -
containing roles - less
pressured environment,
high risk / high reward
more performance based.

Fear of failure,
Perfectionism.
80% is good enough!

Pressure to perform -
different shouldn't be the
same but it is!!

Wed 5/21.

wow! Lord this is a
time to fully trust
in You. You have
given me this time
to rest + more.
Don't let satan steal
my joy.
Things are not going

170

to him and dove I
expect them. And that
is ok.
I surrender all!

Movie was right on.
Saw it twice. Omg God
thank you for using a movie
so special to me.
Thank you for using Grant
to bring me to the movie.
I'm a mess/ a beautiful mess but I'm his
~~put to you~~ masterpiece
and that's enough!

I don't have to do my
life to be happy. It's
not about happiness

Just rest in being who God
created and gifted me
to be. Like the Eagle

I am enough. He is my
enough, my all.
 I don't have to perform
for anyone. —
 I simply need to
rest in this and be
all that I am called to
be. — what is that??

Fulfill my purpose right
here and there now where
I have been placed.

Life is about finding the
meaning and purpose in all
the chaos.

5/22 Casina celebration of life.
 Even in the midst of the storm.
My Jesus is with me —
He is my comforter. He is.
my dependent — in Him I am
dependent. I rest in
knowing Lord you are with
me in the boat.
 I choose to walk by faith

and not by spirit Word
Everything is Awesome
because my Jesus is
in control and not me.
Amazing what you are
going to do.
You can work through these
trials & tribulations with
me.
My path is to go through
the cross so that I can
fully see you Lord.

He will never leave me or
forsake me. Don't put
my comfort in material
things - they will pass
by they will be destroyed
yet my Lord is faithful
and always there for me.

Lord I choose to believe the
away you gave me.

Oe how quickly you
fail.
Elaine/ you receive the
rich period & freedom art
It's ok. I have you
through this. You have
been given the gift of
rest. All is good. You
have been given the gift
to recharge — all is good.
Enjoy this rest day Onie.
You on my Elaine I am
doing such a mighty work
here.
So you are trying to "fix"
you rich Elaine.   ①
Just go with what you
have been given.
All is well. Take the
2 weeks — you have already
taken!
① This time will go by
like a blink of the eye
All will be good.

! Love did you say —
it is rich — you take
rest. Take rest Elaine
it's so!! It is done!

m

Thank you for giving me
the right policy—
    now I know what
I am supposed to be doing.

My issue is that I can't
receive / accept the gift a
rev I have been given.

Just take it / receive it
    embrace it.
    smile "☺" feel my joy +
peace

The gospel of Matthew is
revealing.
    It talks much about
faith.
        pray
    Dear Lord I wish to have
faith as small as a
        mustard seed.
    Lord I trust in You

May Your will be done—
    not mine !!!

Lord what a revelation on
Friday with Christine —
Thank you for using her.

I have so many times
thought I was in control.
How could I possibly
think that I am God.
I thought I was the provider
I had the weight of
trusting everyone, well at
least Kevin and Angela
depended on me. All the
pressure was on me to
perform and meet their
needs. Oh wow!! What a
weight and burden I have
been carrying!
Elaine can't you see
that you are NOT in
control I AM!!
I have brought you
to a place of total
dependence on me
You really have to trust
me on this one Elaine.
With all your mind, heart

and soul. We are going to
get through this. I am
going to carry along in
my arms.
This is a true test of
your faith and trust in
me. Step onto the bridge
and over the cliff. As
much as you can't see
anything. I am there.
Thank you for your
faith and your word.
I need to be reminded daily -
moment by moment.

_____   Tues 5/27

What is my dream?
My dream is to coach /
facilitate / be an amazing
wife + mother + grandmother

From life to dream - need to
get out of the middle.
Why don't dreams come true?
Life just keeps going on.
People who refuse to quite
and don't give up will make it

to the end and go over the
finish line.

Promises of God are for whoever
will.
    I can be in the palace
and come out the pit.

I have a testimony when I pour
the fear. I don't want to
be a ~~moaning~~ moanie.

Isaih 61: Beauty from ashes.

Jesus is an expert at getting
people out of pits.

[Elaine you think kevin is
    not going to make ...
are you playing God Elaine ???]

Victory a God is a walk on an
escalator one step at a time.

Trust God He will work it for
my good and use it for my
benefit. He takes bad stuff and

makes good stuff
My worst enemy today is
my best friend in the future
I'm hanging on through
all I got.

[But Kevin has not been part
of such a big club]

Joseph in prison for 13 years.

God should I be in Florida???
Not yet !!!!! one day is
my time

What men means for harm.
God intends for good.

Dig in bean hills, I am never
quit and and never going to
give up.
Time to come empartca
pw. Zach 7:11-12.
Thank God because in
blood of Christ I have been
released.

Be a prisoner of hope
can't get away from hope.
I won't stop hoping that I
will see change in my life.

Attitude of confidence and
trust.
God will give me double
what I lost. double for my
trouble ☺

Rev. 20:1-3. Satan is
bound in bottomless pit. He
wants to keep me in one.
I will not allow it
Jesus.

Don't get started on victory and
then give up.
Testing times test character
Develop us into people need
to be.

[go for dinner with Kevin tonight]

When have a big vision not
satisfied with little

Whats my vision for better what
I have now??

Need to believe the impossible with
a spark of hope.
I have to pass test.
Don't funk, keep doing whatevers,
to overs
Take same test 200 times.
Maybe need to yield and do
what God wants me to.
God is not going to change
his mind and what he
will continue to do.
Donkey and dirt - shake it off
stand on top of it and
continue on journey.

[You have no idea trailie what
I am work here - don't try to
figure it out + fix it !]

God is faithful in every situation
made up my mind never going to
give up !!!!

In Christ I can have a
brand new beginning.
It's never too late

Lord —
I can learn to do the
right thing, while I'm
hurting to do right thing
~~when~~ even when it
doesn't feel good.

When we are hurting we need to
behave the way we would
if things were going exactly
the way they were supposed
to.

It's amazing how I can do things
that I really don't think I
can.
  I can!! — I need to take
the bridge and step out in
faith.

Have to own my behaviour
and not say I can't help it.
I have the fruit of self-control.

1) when hurting don't go wild
and go wild with intemperance
and have no boundaries.
If I can control the mouth
when hurting. — not say
how I feel but God would
want me to say.
Thank God!! instead of
having a fit.
Thank you God that I can trust
you to take care of this problem.

2) Don't withdraw or isolate
self, pout, pity party —
get depressed and in a pit.
can be pitiful or powerful.
I have to stop feeling sorry
for myself.
Someone is going through
something worse.

3) Don't believe lie that
God is punishing me for
some other sin.
Non business God is in
He forgives are remember
sin no more.

Stop remembering what
God has forgotten.

4) Don't blame God and
be mad at him
I am ~~just~~ Trust God to
give me the very best He
has in mind for me.
Don't get mad at God
because he is not working my
plan.

5) Don't give up and think There
is no way out.
Jesus is way out

6) Don't passively ~~to~~ continue
with injustice
Do good for people. My way
to defeat devil is to do as
much good I can possibly
do. Negate devil balm
by having abundant attitude.
Trust God — God has
a plan for me — he
has a reason.
God doesn't do bad things.

7) Keep your commitments
Keep your word.
Do what few people would do.
Galatians 6:9.
Don't get tired doing whats
right
Am I going to be a person of
My word??

Hang on to integrity. These
times build character —
keep commitments — and
run up and have a fit.
I am growing spiritually and
after baby going to be
one day closer.
I have to go through the
middle. Determinis howlong
it will take me to get there.

When hurting — need to do what is
right — when everything goes
wrong.

I don't have time to
waste time wallowing and
feel sorry about myself.

Time is short + running out!!!
God has me in the right place
at the right time and
Say God I trust You

God ~~crossed out~~ she I give up
too soon

Don't run away from
PS 91:2 something
just because I don't want
to be there.

Say God I trust You I'm
hurting so bad I trust
You Lord.
God is a fair judge and
a God of justice.

I know you have already
forgiven me Lord as I have
asked for forgiveness so many
times. I'm so sorry for
"quitting" and not standing
strong. Now it is my time
to continue to be strong in
my faith Lord and know that you

are a a greate worth here more
than my eyes and mind can
even imagine.
   You are doing and will do
amazing things more than I can
ever imagine and they will
look nothing like I ever
dreamed of.
   I know that I will continue
because I have you Lord.
I have your strength and
your spirit.
   When each little trial comes
by with some information
that goes against everything
that I have imagined I need
to thank you Lord for that
opportunity.
   I don't want to be come
the self-fulfilling prophecy
that I have already played
out in my mind!!
   The Be strong Gianie, stay
strong.
Wow! what a thought
Minds is like CSA !!!

→ Acknowledge the fear.
→ What is going truth
→ listen to hear it, don't discount it
→ Move forward.

Ignore fear / try to counteract it
just becomes bigger.

What focus on give power to.

God box ‾
 → Shoebox, decorate it
 → incense.
 ⇒ loose paper —
  write our control over it /
  influence it.
  Absolutely no control over it
  Physically putting it in a
→ God box.
  Control over some things
 making an intention to do.
  give space to Holy Spirit.
  make it a beautiful ceremony.

Journal : what doing ⎤thoughts / beliefs⎤
  ⎥feelings⎥
  ⎦body sensations⎦

188

- Some movement - every day.
walking etc.

Lamentations 3: 22-23
Send 6/8.
Because of the Lords great love
we are not consumed, for his
compassions never fail.
They are new every morning
Great is your faithfulness.

Thoughts / beliefs
That I may be poor / homeless /
without.
That is a lie from Satan and
I stand on the truth that
my God is my provider. He has
always provided and will
continue to provide.
How many times Lord have
we 'been without' or wondering
how to make the next bill
waiting for the next paycheck
and you came through.
I do really believe Lord
that with you all things
are possible.

Does that mean Elaine that
you will surrender the
decision to move to
Florida.
Yes Lord I surrender —
and I bow for you to ponder
The sign that that without
a shadow or a doubt, I
can tell You are in it Lord.
I do pray Lord for my
husband Kevin. Lord I
pray that he is diligently
seeking your face. I pray
for a wake up call for him
to see your power Lord.
Lord I don't know his heart
only You do. Lord I
pray that he is listening to
you that he is taking time
to seek you out and
hear your quiet still voice.
That he will receive the
knowing that only comes
from hearing and being
in touch with you. —
Listening to you!
Wow Lord I feel like my life

will never be the same again. It won't Claire. It will be so different, quite different than you can ever to have imagined. In a way that you will see my hand over it all.

You will be in a place a place and contentment Claire.

You will be so strong and courageous and bold.

Now Claire is something going to happen to her in my Brazil trip? No!! Don't be crazy!!

Lord what do you want from me?

Claire I simply want you to rest and trust in me. You know I will never leave you or forsake you. You know I have your back.

Claire you still think you are not good enough / smart enough. You know that you are my precious daughter and I love you so much. You don't have to concern yourself about others.

If I am for you who can be

against you.

I totally get it Lord.
I need your strength to rely
for Jesus to be the center
of my life. I have that say!!
now Lord — I lose Snowy
and how all this in the
same year. What is it all
about!!

You know Lord you
would have not gone to
Chicago — maybe Snowy would
have ? I'll be here ??
NO! NO! NO! That is a lie —
it was Snowy's time.
Oh Lord — please give me
direction, & wisdom.
I think you know Lord —
you need to release and
let go.

6/10/
Lord why do I not trust? Elaine
that is great that you question
this. The first step is acknowledge
it. Elaine your lack of trust is
that you have tried to be in

control in the past. Now it is
all as your control and I am in
this. Now Elaine you Marcy
have trust me and know that
I am in this. This Elaine is
the biggest step of faith that
you have taken. It is going
to be ok — Marcy don't care
if you live in Florida or Alt
what I am about is that you
trust me and believe I am your
provider. — I know that you are
Lord. I need to put my
cares and worry at the foot of
the cross and give it to you.
Today is a new day Lord.
A day in which I can with
your strength take a step forward
it the direction in which you
want me to go. I love you
Lord.
Elaine listen to me — it is
going to be ok — you trust me
and listen to me and it will
be ok — TRUST ME!!
Lord I don't want want to be
like the Israelites wandering around

in circles in 40 years because
to my unbeing lord I do believe
you. I trust you lord

The sun is shining on this
page as I write. Lord you are
my sunshine.

Elaine no longer keep leaning
down. Rise up. Don't fear and
keep your eyes focused on me
Elaine.

Elaine This is a new day. You are
able to do and get through this day
because you have my strength.
You can't do it on your own.
You can only do it with me.
Thank you lord. I rejoice in
you and all your provisions.

My world has turned upside
down lord. And that is ok.
Elaine. I am in this world
with you. I am here for you
Oh Elaine you have to let go
of these chairs that are
holding you down. Break free
so that you can see the
blessings I have for you. You
are my amazing daughter and

you know that I only want is
my best for you — may not be
your best.

Elaine as you prepare to move
to Florida Satan will continually
attack you. I want you to put
on your armor as God so that
you are protected. Continue to
think the truth, speak the
truth and act out the truth.

It is going to difficult but
again you can do it with my
strength. You are my wonderful
child you sit on my lap and I
will cherish you again.

Oh what a sweet time this
has been. I know it has been
hard but how much we have
come to know each other more
intimately. Now Elaine you
need to trust me. move on and
take a step forward today.

Sign the paperwork from the
landlord for your house.

Look at houses and ask Tim to
look at them. See how I bring
him to you ☺ — Yes I love you

are so in the defeat.
What is the armor of God.
Belt of truth buckled round waist
Breastplate of righteousness
Feet fitted with Readiness that
Comes from the gospel of peace.
Shield of faith to extinguish
burning arrows
Helmet of salvation
Sword of the spirit — is the
word of God.
Keep praying.

Phillipians 3:21.
Who by His power enables him
to bring everything under
control.

You are in control Lord. How
can I ever doubt that?

Lord I surrender all this day to
you let me live moment by
moment.
Phillip. 3:13-14 Forgetting
what is behind and straining
towards what is ahead.

press on toward the good to visin
the prize for which Christ has
called me.

2 Thess. 3:16
Now may the one Lord do place
him say give you peace at all
times and in every way. The Lord
be with all of you.

6/10 pm

Feeling a lot calmer today
well this afternoon after my
crying out to the Lord this
morning.
I am taking one step at a
time, deep breathe Lord 1
believe you want us to go
to Florida and then if that is
not meant to be you will
absolutely close the door - byway!

6/11

Lord first you say go to Florida
and then you say to me today
stay in Charlotte - you will
miss the blessings of Florida,
but receive more different blessing here.

4:30 Tuesday

One thousand gifts   6/10/14
Eucharist - Grace -
Give thanks

1. Today - being able to rest
   under a tree in the shade -
   the first time I have done
   this in the 8 years I have
   lived in this house.
2. Being able spend time with
   Olga.
3. Traceys wrinkles - the time
   as age and the stories
4. feeling sun on my face
5. Being able to drive.
6. Friends who support me.
7. Birds singing
8. Being able to walk around.
9. Rain drops falling from a
   tree line I drove
10. Spending time with Olga.
11. Being able to drive.
12. Church and kids
13. Brian Johnson listening
14. Josephine going to Georgia.
    └ wonderful daughter.
15. Family still keeping in touch.
16. Farmers day.

17. ar around Beatty little girl shouting "daddy". thba father You are my daddy.
18. listening to the ducks.
19. The storm is about to come through - I hear the thunder. Your creation is amazing.
20. Children win dog that loved like snowy.
21. The mild evening
22. A pretty full nights sleep
23. Feeling of peace about staying or going.
24. I ask for some help for company - Jennife londa the house wed night
25. what an I day tonight Then Jen Landa turns up.
26. listen to crickets and chirping.
27. Picture of birds in nests all tucked up for night.
28. Grace life
29. our dear Lord Jesus Christ and His grace and mercy!!

What is that all about Lord.
Elaine its your choice.
You can go or stay. For me
its about peace I will use
you and bless you wherever
you live.
The big thing about staying
in Manston is will Kevin
still be able to go to
CUFC?? Probably not sure
is where Papa only.
Oh dear Lord please give
me clarity.

There are now a lot of confusion
00 why am I confused.
2) its me analyzing.
Lord I need to rest in you
and what you are telling me.
What is Ps. 131.

I called and you answered
Elaine you really have
you are going to think
Don't fight it. Embrace
it you are wasting time
each day is precious.

<u>Pack rats</u>
855 202 3901. X1054   Debbie $3000.

John, meet tomorrow — before 1pm?

Romans 15:13. May be God a your
hope so fill you with all joy and
peace in believing so that by
the power as the Holy Spirit you
may abound in hope.

John I would love to meet
tomorrow and speak
face to face. What time
are you coming in? after 3pm.

215 446 0143   359842
                                  —

Top Performer — Comp.

OMG — why did I leave my
tour!! CRAZY, CRAZY.
    CRAZY!!!!!!!!) !)

← well thats set me up for
counselling!!!

- Pride / myself idol
- my perfectionism
- performance
- achievement
- pray through this
- I don't have to be the best
- Lord is merciful because
who is like Jesus.

Lord give me the grace to know
I'm not perfect. It's ok to
make mistakes. I'm only
human.
Faulty role I was successful
doing it hard in glore –
really using my gifting. Was
I doing it in my own strength?
Each morning did I wake up
thanking Jesus – no.

This is not a trust issue. It's
an issue about Elaine and
her pride and perfectionism.

Don't make impulsive decisions
use mind don't be just true
give it to God. – and expect him

to do. He has given us a
mind - need to reason.
We are going to make mistakes
and that is ok rest in the lords
grace and mercy.
Need to be thinking of The
eternal kingdom perspective and
where is our focus??

(HUMBLE)

God is not a Genie in a bottle.
and to be so directive.

6/12

Lord the sleeping pills didn't work.
But thank you for the time with Olga
Lord now I give the
move to Florida to you. I give
my job to you.

Think about plans going back to
work - client service
    - LTD - tour.
    - facilitated learning - Glanse.
    She said not easily support

plans to move back to LTP? → speak to Lisakirstein what about tow in POT — closes next week.

Florida when 55 ??? give time to save and make clear plans. maybe you retire there ???

I am fearfully and wonderfully made this can is to long Him glory as I live out a witness before a watching world

John 10:10 I came that they may have life and have it abundantly.

John still coming to see me. Wow.

God your plans are better than my dreams.

What are my options??
- GTD - Too, facilitated learning.
- CS.
-

have a mindset of curiosity.
Ask questions - don't get
stuck into own thinking
Not helpful.
What is it Lord you
have for me.
Peace, Joy and know
that I am your abundance.
Look to me, trust and
not yourself.

6/14.

~~Pan~~ Am I a human having a
christian experience
Am I christian having a
human experience.

Phillipians 4 : 4 - 8.

Whatever I do does not make a
difference - not make this day
or ruin this day

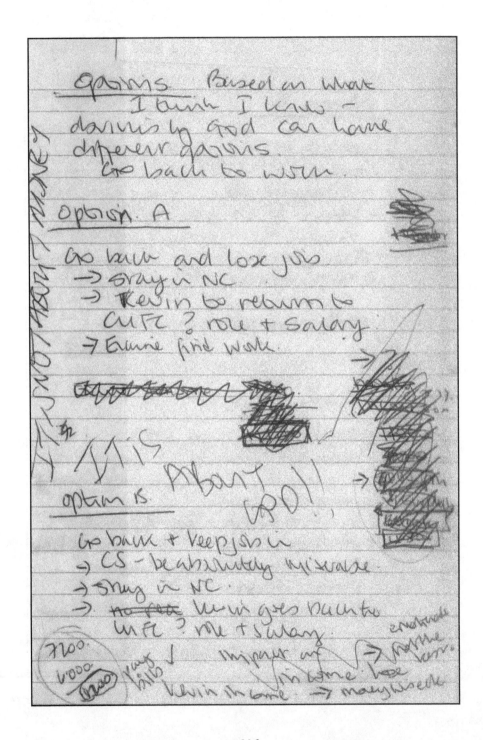

Monday June 9th. 4:30 pm.

3:30 June 2 counsellor

What does this say about me
give myself permission

Blocks / permissive - breathe
Give it to God

John + Lisa

Follow my passion in
LTD impacts many more
their only one at time
their service is challenging,
transition has been
difficult - we know I
have been wanting to end
transition to their services
and this has confirmed it
What are my options?
There is a role for Jenn
Gale team. - what
Are there other options?

6/16 Carmel Beatty Park.

God is more concerned with my
focus on Him and not on
me.
Wow I feel a peace about it
really doesn't matter about staying
or go to. I know that I can to
Florida, I know that I can stay.

— Fill in the paperwork to.
— Look at rentals for 2 days.
— Apply for jobs.

Phil 4:19.
And my God will supply every need
of yours (mine) according to his
riches in glory in Christ Jesus.

It would be very humbling to
Stay in Charlotte.
Proverbs 22:4.
The result of humility and
the fear of the Lord is
wealth, honor & life.

God I want to put you first
in my life because I know
your ways are the best.
 Every step I take, I
breathe I make is you Lord.
Lord let my focus be on you
first and not on me ☺

   me ☹ you ☺

I'm debating about a salary
reduction—plus also about the job.
A job that is not fully in my
offering but one I could likely do.
Then I get a call from Bethany
at GLI asking to raise support.

What do you think Lord ??

Tow	F/T.
→ one year.	⇒ "permanent"
⇒ opp to explore role.	→ not sure its my passion.
⇒ comp remains	⇒ reduction in comp. $20.8k
→ less stability	⇒ more stability
→. still on fence.	⇒ decisive.
→ start immediately.	→ start late -home ↳ go back CS.

Speak to counsellor re job
—
Go home — sign form.
           — check out some rentals
           — wash dishes — clean up.

Write Kevin list of jobs to do.
Decisions needed this week.
           — Grant Job
           — Florida.

6/17
Dear Lord thank you for giving
me some peace yesterday I pray
That continues today.
   The news about my job is bitter
sweet as I will apply for the
full time role but that process
takes a while and so I will
likely need to do some client
service work in the meantime as
I will need to be billable.—
doesn't give me great joy but
you know Lord if I drop my
pride and you will I know me
it will be by your grace That
we can get through this

As I read my previous journals
I had already identified the
pride issue - Thanks for using
the counselor to confirm this.
It was painful but true
Please keep checking me in this
area. It has been a life long
struggle and will be difficult to
do but I can do it with your
strength.
What to do today - What any
reviews that may come through
but I think you know by now
desire that you are not leaving
you are staying in Charlotte
Especially after the news of your
job. Is that right Lord.
Florida is a new office - and yes
desire you any was loss forward
there plus partner who is here
there
    See if you can meet Traci -
go on elliptical for 10 mins.
Go to Starbucks / Panera to
read - get out do have.
    Fear of God should be
greater than the fear of man.

6/17
Afternoon 6/17 after counseling
session.

Wow Lord, you confirmed that
it is ok to stay in Charlotte.
We simply need to communicate
that decision.

It will be hard at first for
Kevin & I – maybe, your providence
that he is going to Brazil.
We know (and you will make it
clear) when is the right time
to move to Florida.

Lets see where Angela does
eventually end up on land –
it could be somewhere totally
different.

Lets see if Kevin can apply
for other jobs and do some
research –

Lord I do feel calmer now, my
legs are not shaking – now to
tell Kevin. Dear Lord, prepare
his heart for this news.

Dear Lord protect our marriage
through this.

Dear Lord, let Kevin see you at
work in this and what he can

also learn from this situation and
any issues that he has he
to deal with. May he pray
search my heart......
Lord I know that I have not let
you down. Lord, I know that
you will be with you me.
Lord I ask for your grace as
I make mistakes and drop my
perfectionism and pride
and impulsive decision making
Wow lord this journey is
certainly not over and it will
won't be until I am in heaven
with you dear Lord.
2 know I will continue to be
broken as the onion layers are
being peeled back and you are
going deep into the core of
lifelong issues that I am dealing
with.
This most definitely has not
been a waste of time Lord -
wow how I have come to know
you and your sovereignty and also
me and how I need to humble myself
before you. Now I'm tired and

thats exactly where you want me
to be dependent on you and
not me!!
Thank you so much for being
my lord & Savior.

Sun 6/2?

- Told Kevin but the
when the counsellor told
me that heart says
- Should go to France -
"But not now" -
I think the but not now
was me my fear Lord.
(But is the truth. Yes,
Lord - but is "bullshit").
Its the first thing that comes
to heart is true.
- Called counsellor for
emergency appt on Friday
truth maybe decision to go
to France - Terrifying -
Change need answers -
perfectionism.
Should not be fear no man
lie a man
obedience better than sacrifice.
Fear of going back to work.

Not be a perfectionist.
Whoever said that what you
should do + know → know that
should go to Florida → shining
in my heart.
Use encouragement. — speak life.

Habit to speak words of life not
death.
Christians give life and grace
not take away the.

God way no sin that in
entire whatever your choice.

I want Holy Spirit to love living
inside as me.
Be obedient to Lord + husband

Let yes be yes and your no be no.

God forgave me. I was a
wreck, before and after saved.
But God by His grace changed me.
He forgives me all the time
Need to walk in forgiveness.
Freedom

walk in freedom → — forgiveness.
Greatest hindrance in healing
moving forward unforgiving
spirit and a bitter heart.

Hebrews 11:12

Fixing eyes on what is
2 Cor. 4:18 — seen ↓

This is
temporary

What is unseen is eternal.

Fix my eyes on Jesus

Today is a new day.
Thank you JESUS JESUS
JESUS JESUS JESUS
for your peace and your
power Jesus JESUS Jesus
you JESUS ARE TRUTH
my focus is on you —
only You Jesus Jesus
JESUS JESUS JESUS
JESUS JESUS.

I lay down at foot of
cross, decision where
Orlando. Jesus you are

amazing. This is not
about me this is
about You!! God/
Jesus / HOLY SPIRIT.

You and me, You JESUS!!
Jesus JESUS!!

My God is mighty,
my God is strong
than any one !!!/!!

Jesus Jesus Jesus Jesus.
Jesus Jesus Jesus
Jesus Jesus.

Thank you Jesus —
Yes the move was all
about me and my plans
not your plans —
In your perfect timing Jesus
you will provide the path
— It doesn't matter what
others think or say. I
stand firm in you Jesus
Jesus Jesus Jesus Jesus
but You butt has has been Lead

6/25-

I sit in Jesus lap.
Safe and secure in Jesus
lap. He is my safety
He is my security.
Jesus you make bones
beautiful.
I have your confidence
Jesus Jesus Jesus Jesus
Jesus Jesus Jesus Jesus
Jesus you are my confidence.
You Jesus are my
strength You Jesus are
my glory You Jesus are
my all. It's all about
You Jesus its not
about me.
Jesus let me rest in
your arms — the cutie girl
with the little face—
Jesus you are my all.

Wow how I have lived
under law all this time
when proud, scared,
need!!! — You have
my freedom Jesus, Jesus
Jesus, Jesus, Jesus.

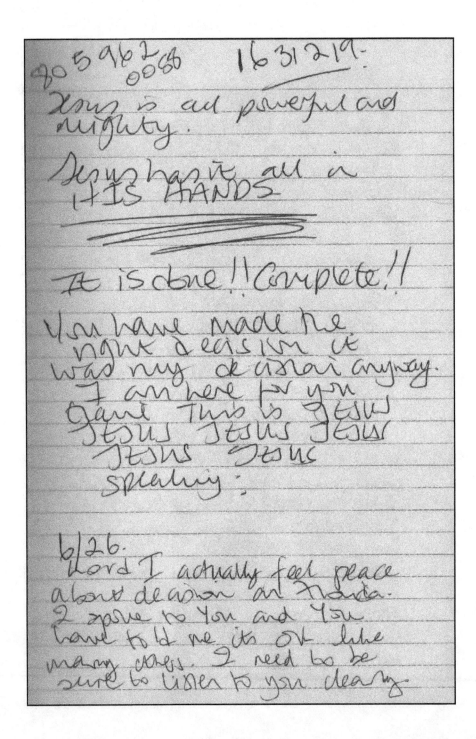

805 962 0080   1631219.

Xmas is all powerful and mighty.

Jesus has it all in HIS HANDS

It is done!! Complete!!

You have made the right decision it was my decision anyway. I am here for you Janet This is JESUS JESUS JESUS JESUS JESUS JESUS speaking.

6/26.
Lord I actually feel peace about decision on Nanda. I gave to You and You have told me its ok like many others. I need to be sure to listen to you clearly.

A psychiatrist. Oh my!!
I know I have issues
because do what they say
about me.
What do you think Lord??
Elaine it's time to me.
Try to stop taking
control and let me
flow through you. —
There is freedom in me.
Elaine the cute girl
sitting on my lap
I just simply want
her to be at peace!!
Peace in JESUS JESUS
JESUS JESUS.

Why do you put yourself
in stressful situations??
Because always looking
for something else — why?
because do any competence.
Any competence + confidence
comes from Jesus Christ.
I have to learn and be
open to growing and
developing. It is true

221

Gave to show that you
are capable. That you
are able to do this —
Why — Because its not
You have its ME — JESUS
JESUS JESUS JESUS JESUS.
JESUS JESUS JESUS
JESUS JESUS JESUS.

Freedom have from S —
you have it because
you have my authority
Gave — You have me
in You — and thats all
that matters!!!

Jesus ~~I have~~ remove
the lie of ~~the~~ not trusting.
In You I do TRUST and give
all my cares + worries

6/23.

wow where has time gone.
Lord I thank you for this
time with you. I have asked
for forgiveness about grace life
and thank you for filling me
with life and pointing me
to Maria.

I don't have to look at my
job, family to define me.
I am because You are in
me. I am because He is.
Lord I know your perfect
will is being done in my life

I am so sorrowful about not
living out the gift fully.
You I know you know how
painful that is for me Lord.
Lord I ask you to heal
those heart places.

The Spirit gives life the flesh
counts for nothing. John 6:

Lord how do you want me to
respond to this situation I put

it is your hands.

Elaine I have you in my hands
you are sitting on my lap.
I want you to finally surrender
all. know that you do believe
in me and now its time to
experience me. Thank you Jesus.
wow. This has been quite
a journey.

God is God a gizzionlth chance.
Thank You Jesus!!!!

Replace feelings with truth.

Feeling of deep sorrow.
- Fear of what I did wrong.
- Thoughts all makes me feel scared.
- Feel like at a place of no return.

Truth - my lord will never leave me nor forsake me.
- Yes He disciplines but in love. He is not a vengeful God.

Need to consider eternity and His big picture not what I can see only now.

Deeper hurt the deeper the pain. Jesus is the only drug He satisfies
This is to No emotional hurt physical hurt requires drugs.

God wants us to deal with the sin and ALL OF IT - He don't

want us to have consequences!

Isaih 46 . I am God, and there
               is no other
          I am God and there is none
           like me.
          I make known the end
     from the beginning.
       from ancient times what
     is still to come.
     I say . my purpose will stand
     and I will do all that
          I please.

In Him I live and breathe
and have a being.
God actively works in me
to bring me to full potential.

Listen to Jesus the outcome
is holy living is the
eternal life of Christ
lived through us

Jesus and grace give freely
life.

Christ is in me HE is
my life.

I am in Christ I have a
new identity which
loves righteous living

I can choose death or
life —

I CHOOSE LIFE!!

CHRIST I choose you to
live in me!!!

Truth sets us free.
Sin/lies keep us in
bondage.

Truth is Christ!!!!!!!

Holy Spirit deals with thoughts.

1 John. Put God 1st — Don't dwell
on other things
I know Lord that I am Yours
I will never forget my day I

Salvation. Thank you so much JESUS CHRIST for being my Lord and Savior. For giving your one and only Son for us for me. That He died to make me righteous and to take away my sin past, present and future.

Do not listen to the world Elaine. Listen to me — your one and only TRUE GOD JESUS CHRIST who loves you so much. I am so sorry and I truly confessed. for my sin of running to the world and others seeking advice and not running to you. Will you please take me back?

Elaine I have never left you!! You left me for a little while. I am so thankful Elaine that you are coming back. I know you used Cathy & Barb to encourage me and Aunt to turn me away. Lord, please continue to give me discernment.

Let me confess why I gave
up the gift:
1) I wanted to go on the
Hudson coaching program
and have the company fund it
— which they did but I
did not attend because I
was sick!!
2) Too proud to stay in role —
boring, not challenging —
Forgetting the reason why I
took the role in the first place —
You gave it to use my
gifts not passions and to
impact so many people!
— now I'm not using my
gifting and not impacting
many people.
3) For some weird reason
Thought I had to be back
in CS to a
more permanent role to be
in Orlando!! — Screwed
up thinking
4) To get vacations in!!!
Lots of lies there. Game.
Renounce the lies and I will

replace them with truth.

The biggest lie is that I
thought I had control, and
could be like God!!!!
Oh wow what a huge lie —
I know that You are Jesus
Christ omniscient, omipotent.
Wow I am so repentant Lord as
that action. I know you
will discipline mercy.
I know You love me 1/ 50000
much!!!!!! :-)

Hold on to my truth Elaine
how I do still love you. You
are no longer of the world, You
are mine, Jesus CHRIST!!! I
believe that my Lord Jesus Christ
wow what revelations!!!

The Lord disciplines and
it is painful — but thankfully
it means He loves me.
He is my father, my duel,
my Abba Father.

The Lord is my helper, I will
not be afraid..
   What can man do to me??

If I live under grace
instead of enemy law I
will have victory in this life.

Can't outrun God!! AMEN!

Sin increases through self-
righteousness. —
   Forgive me I confess Lord
of my self righteousness.
   Wow I have been so bad,
however, I am thankful that
you reveal this to me now
in the powerful name of
Jesus Christ — our Lord and
Savior.

I am a Saint not a sinner.

Oh wow Lord I know I have
not wasted time — what a
refining process.

I want to listen to You
JESUS — Finally —
I want freedom to live
righteously. Lord oh my
Goodness. I need you.
like never before
Elaine you have me, I
have always been here 🙂

Thank You Jesus for your life
and freedom in You.
Elaine do you believe it —
YES I DO LORD!!
Lord I need you so much.
Elaine I am already yours.
and you are mine.
Trust in me and know
the truth!! Lord You are
truth. Oh my how I
missed You Lord?!!

Father GLORIFY YOUR NAME
THIS IS NOT ABOUT ME
IT IS ABOUT YOU.

Its all about You and
not me!! Jesus my lord & savior.

Ps. 13 5+6.
But I trust in your
unfailing love
My heart rejoices in your
salvation
I will sing to the lord
For He has been good to me.

Elaine
on lap

God will use circumstances
for my good. I don't have
to fear
Interpret life through God.
Trust in Him. I do trust
in You my dear LORD
JESUS CHRIST SON OF
THE ONE + ONLY GOD.

TAKE A STEP ELAINE —
one step at a time —
trust me Jesus Christ

God is:
✓ LOVING
✓ ACCEPTING
✓ ALWAYS THERE
✓ FORGIVING
✓ KIND
✓ GOOD

God is much larger then our problems, what me focus on becomes larger then life

GOD YOU ARE MY FOCUS – GOD I ~~KEEP~~ ~~WANT~~ GET TO HAVE YOU as my LORD + SAVIOR. All these weeks focus been in wrong place. FORGIVE ME.

God (just wants a relationship) thats all a relationship

Not to things out of fear. Do it out of Gods love for ~~us~~ me. ~~His response~~ I am responding to His love for me.

I need to get to enjoy His
freedom through His
acceptance of me + His
grace.

God is everlasting.

God is Sovereign Jesus Christ
is sovereign Sovereign.
God is sovereign. God is
Sovereign. God is sovereign
my faith may be weak
but not gone.
my faith is strong and
strong. my faith in
Jesus Christ is strong.
and strong – my faith in
Jesus Christ, Jesus Christ,
Jesus Christ.

Love of Jesus Christ of God
The is done good. won by god
by Jesus Christ my Lord
+ Saw won by Jesus Christ
my lord + won by by Jesus
Christ, GOD IN THE
NAME OF JESUS CHRIST

JESUS CHRIST JESUS CHRIST
JESUS CHRIST JESUS
CHRIST JESUS CHRIST
JESUS CHRIST JESUS CHRIST
GOD IS MY SAVIOUR HE IS
HERE FOR ME HE IS MY
LORD + SAVIOUR HE LOVES
ME SOO SOOO OOO SOO MUCH
JESUS CHRIST JESUS CHRIST
JESUS CHRIST GOD GOD
GOD GOD GOD GOD
JESUS CHRIST JESUS CHRIST
JESUS CHRIST JESUS CHRIST
GOD GOD GOD GOD
GOD IS MY LORD AND SAVIOUR.

God is UNIQUE.

So do not fear, for I am with
you;
Do not be dismay for I am
you God, (Jesus Christ)

God the Father, God the Son
and God the Holy Spirit
Son = Jesus Christ

God is :
The almighty one.
God most high
God who sees.
The all sufficient one.
Lord, master.
Lord self existent one.
He is life and source of life.
God is I AM.
LORD - self-existent one.
I am that I am.
Lord will provide
Lord heals.
Lord my banner.
Lord my banner.
Lord sanctifies you.
The Lord is my helper
I will not fear.
What can man do to me.

The Lord sanctifies you.
Let not your heart be troubled
you believe in God, believe
also in me.
Lord will never leave me
or forsake me.

Lord is peace.
I am accepted, significant
and loved.
Lord of hosts.
For the battle is the Lords.
In and of ourselves we are
inadequate. I am
Lord is my shepherd
I am a the sheep in His
pasture – Jesus Christ.
Lord is our Righteousness.
Right standing with God.
He is av identity
Lord who is present.
He is in both the Old Testament
and the New Testament.

Trust and He will bring it to
pass.
Do not fret – it causes harm.

Wait on the Lord

Steps of a good man are
ordered by the Lord and
He delights in His way

He Elaine
Though ~~the~~ fails He (Elaine)
shall not be utterly
cast down
For the Lord uphold him
(Elaine) with His hand.

He is ever merciful.

Gods relationships style is
different.

He relates out as fullness as His
character.
   — Unconditionaly
   — Grace-fully
   — Based on who He is

I choose to receive You
Lord Jesus as my life and
I believe in You Jesus my
Lord and saviour
I want to and get to
live for your glory Jesus.

Don't live in the falsehood
of my circumstances
Live in the freedom of the

truth of Jesus and his character and how much He loves me and He will never leave me nor forsake me.

Jesus is the true Shepherd who seeks His lost sheep

Compassion and mercy of God's is new each morning.

Come boldly to the throne of grace that we may obtain mercy and find grace in time of need.

Jesus renews spiritual vitality

My focus is on Jesus, Jesus Jesus, Jesus, Jesus, Jesus Jesus, Jesus, Jesus Jesus Jesus, Jesus, Jesus, Jesus, Jesus, Jesus, Jesus, Jesus, Jesus, Jesus, Jesus, Jesus Jesus, Jesus Jesus Jesus, Jesus, Jesus.

Jesus our God the Father,
God the Son Jesus Christ,
God the Holy Spirit

Jesus, Jesus, Jesus.

Receive, Believe & Act a
Jesus, Jesus, Jesus,
Jesus, Jesus, Jesus,
Jesus, Jesus, Jesus,
Jesus, Jesus, Jesus,
Jesus, Jesus, Jesus,
Jesus, Jesus, Jesus,
Jesus, Jesus, Jesus
Jesus Jesus Jesus,
Jesus Jesus, Jesus
Jesus, Jesus, Jesus,
Jesus has won battle,
period. done / complete! //
That is it over & done !!

Jesus has won !!
It is finished Jesus
has won.
Jesus has won !!
Jesus has won !! Jesus
has won !! Jesus has won !!

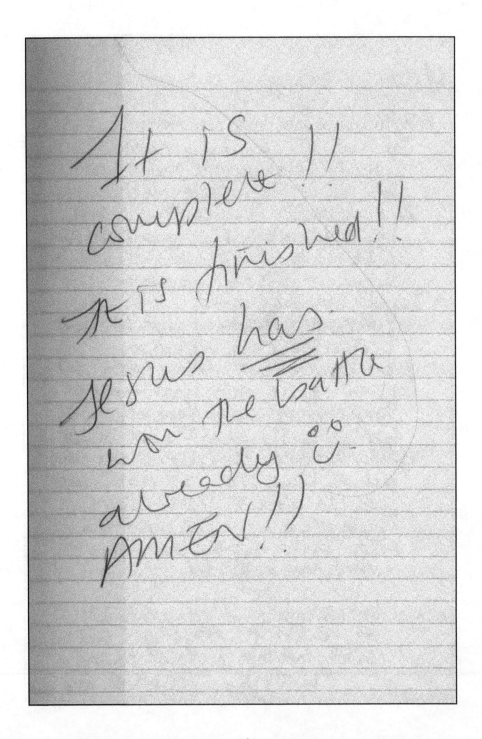

It is
complete !!
It is finished !!
Jesus has
won the battle
already ☺
AMEN !!

6/28:

All this is for His Christs
Glory. This has never
been about me —
It has been been about
me getting close to Him.
and living the inside/out
life.

Lord Jesus Christ,
Please I know I am forgiven
I confess my actions
and heart has been
that of the rich young ruler.
I am so oso so so so
sorry. Lord I want and need
your name to be glorified in
all of this. This is not about
me its about You living
the life.
You will live your life in
me, as me!!

Oh wow!! I'm so sorry
to Kevin + Angela for
all what I put them
through. I'm not too

late Elaine — to change
decision about Florida.!!
Kevin will not budge
now Lord.
Elaine remember. I am
God and you are not.!!
Give it one more try.
No Satan go away. —
You are trying to mess up
my marriage. — Oh Elaine.

Satan doesn't care if you move
or don't move.

Elaine you were focused on
external and not internal.
From first day with Nancy
you felt unsettled why go
to her? —

~~Continue to g~~
In ~~thanks~~ everything give
thanks; for this is Gods
will for you in christ
Jesus.!!

4/29.

"The spirit of God is in union with my spirit - AMEN!!

Place of perfect stillness & and quietness which simply is where we know what we know.

Don't judge reality by whats happening at the soul level - my feelings - may miss God.

God speaks through spirit in silence.

Show us what it is meant to know spirit so not confused and controlled by feelings

lie - dirty, unworthy, shameful
hiding in the dark -
running away.

Replace Truth:
- I AM WORTHY.
- I AM CLEAN
- I AM WASHED WITH BLOOD
  OF JESUS.
- I AM WHITE AS SNOW

I am in union with Christ.
I am because He is.

You meant it for evil
But ~~crossed out~~ God made
it for good.

How my circumstances seem
so bad to me — But
God is my sufficiency, He
is my all. My peace in the storm
But God is... my provider.
I am Holy and blameless
in His sight and beyond
reproach.

God uses storm to get
back into Spirit →
That is what this has
been about [not] my union
with Christ — but His
union with me — It's
all about Him and
not about me!

As believer regenerated at
salvation no part of me
body or soul is truly
captive to Satan.
He is my anti-Christ.
Satan can't dwell spirit
I am in union with
Christ!!

Union of His spirit with
my spirit.

I will never hunger or thirst
for I have Christ.

This is my total spirit sufficiency

Elaine is crucified with Christ
Nevertheless Elaine lives
Yet not Elaine but Christ
lives in me, and the life
which Elaine now lives in
the flesh Elaine live by
faith in the Son of God
who loved me and gave
himself for Elaine.

Colossians 2:15.
Having disarmed principalities
and powers. He made a public
spectacle of them, triumphing
over them.

7/2. — Wow — a month has passed
— a second in your time Lord!
I feel at a rest and peace
in my spirit Lord, you are
in control — my focus is on
you — and what you have for
me next. But focus on
today.
Jackie Hilderbrand Lord?
Elaine you know Tob is the
right way — trust me.

You have applied for job.
However that can change —
or did you say find the
will this.
Elaine let your Yes be Yes
and No be No. — don't
come across wishy / washy.
and double minded.
There is no right or wrong in
my economy — just learn
to trust me Elaine.

Elaine trust me. I have it
don't try to fix things —
You can't Jackie and

Oh how this has helped me
become secure in You dear
Lord. Really Elaine?

When the next storm comes
which will be soon — stand
firm in me Elaine.
As they said at camp
Think / Pray / Respond.

6/6.

Oh Lord I went back to Nancy
and she is presenting psychiatry??
Elaine I love you when
will you learn to listen to
me.

Why did you show Nancy
text from Diana — that was
totally out of context.

Take a stand for me Elaine.
You have meds now are they
helping? — NO!! The
medication isn't going to chay
with meds — its your belief
Elaine and you strong trust
in me.
Yes you have messed up
your body by playing round
with meds — remember you
are not me Elaine — you
are not God!!

Elaine I will let you
get out of this one.

My biggest fear is the
what if and if only

rest in me Elaine and have
peace.—
Peace beyond all
understanding →
I am yours and you are
mine.

Lord, I know this is as
a result of me lying and
playing God. I have repented
so many times for that —
now I choose Lord to move on
and for you to guide my
path and show me the
right words to say. In a
way that You want
my integrity and character
to be built. I
surrender message communicate
to you —
Oh the wage of sin is
death! I am so thankful
for your redemptive power
Lord.
I know in my heart of
hearts you will never leave
me nor forsake. Oh Lord

the crisis as what it could
have been like saddens me
I know that you love me and
will get me through this as you
live in me — Thank you
Jesus for being alongside me
each and every moment of
each and every day.

Rejoice in the Lord always and
again I say rejoice!!

I only have You now Lord.
→ where do I go from here?
Back in my lap Lord.
Enemy has been defeated!!

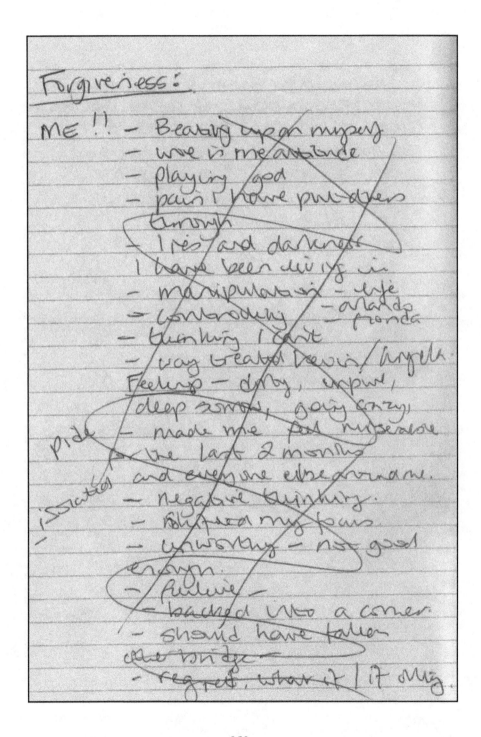

Forgiveness:

ME !! — Beating up on myself
       — woe is me attitude
       — playing god
       — pain I have put others
         through
       — lies and darkness
         I have been living in
       — manipulation — wife
       — controlling — Orlando
                        — Fronda
       — thinking I can't
       — way I treated Kevin/Angela.
Feelings — dirty, impure,
         deep sorrow, going crazy,
pride — made me feel miserable
       the last 2 months
isolated and everyone else around me.
       — negative thinking.
       — blamed my fears.
       — unworthy — not good
enough.
       — failure —
       — backed into a corner.
       — should have fallen
off the bridge —
       — regret, what if / if only.

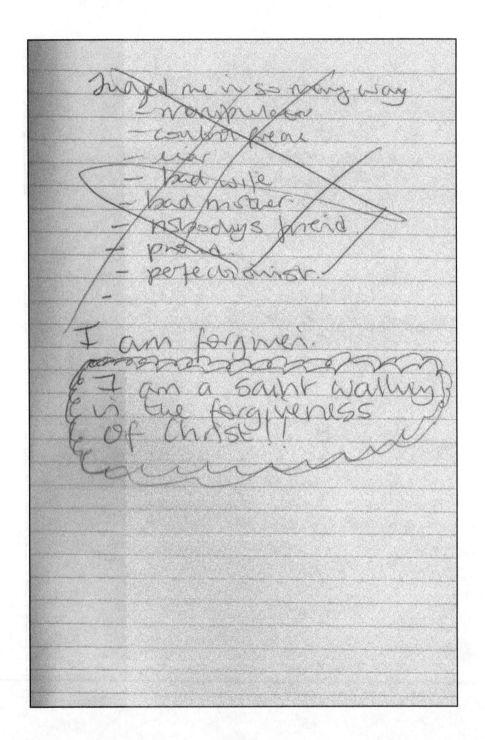

P33.
Shout for Joy in the Lord
- Regardless of circumstances
- I am Righteous.
- Praise befits the upright
- Praise and give Thanks from my heart.
- Sing a new Song.
- Loud shouting
- Our God is a God of Victory in my life
- Shout unto God.
- Jesus set me free
- God has brought freedom.
- Never do Israel.

Keep hope in Jesus Only hope in the name of Jesus. Can have Joy in Jesus.

Lord,
Shelter me under your wing.

#23

Lord, lord, what have I done!!
Your timing is perfect —
You chasten me and
discipline me. — To see
the error of my ways.
Lord — why do I keep on doing
this?? Because

Lord I know you are the
ruler over ~~everything~~ You
are in ~~control~~ not me.

Forgive me for my double
mindedness, forgive me for all
I confess that I continue
to be focussed on some
others — and shift my focus
to you. —

God plan should be the first not the last option.

God I confess my focus shifting.

God give me the courage to be honest as much as it will likely affect my reputation, job etc nothing to none as this is in comparison to losing you. - I don't want to lose you.

Courage to contact the psychiatrist tell him
① Not fill in the paperwork but

How do I stop this insanity??
You can't Elaine — only
by trusting in me will you
break free from this —
Yes as the world would
put it — go cold turkey !!!
— Wake up right now.
before you go any deeper Elaine.

— It wasn't about Jas or a
date or anything like that
its about do You know truly
know who I am and my
love, grace, mercy, power,
— I know love your power,
I also know that you love
me as your child, friend,
daughter,

Who should I pray for and
encourage
- Traci Griffith + family,
Pray for baby, pray for the

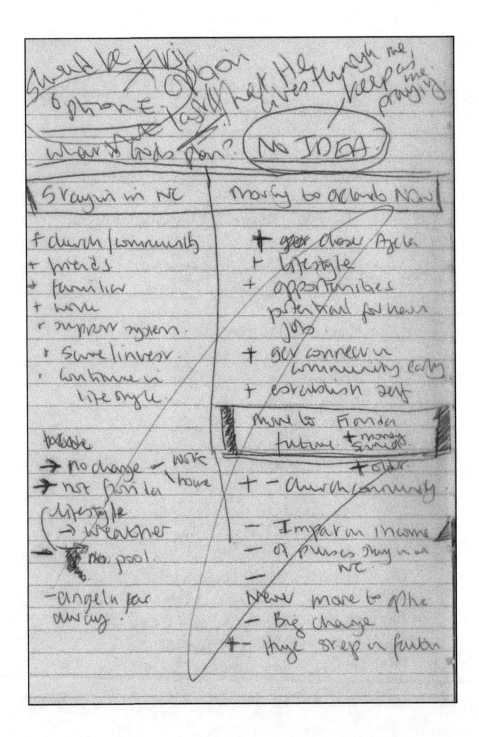

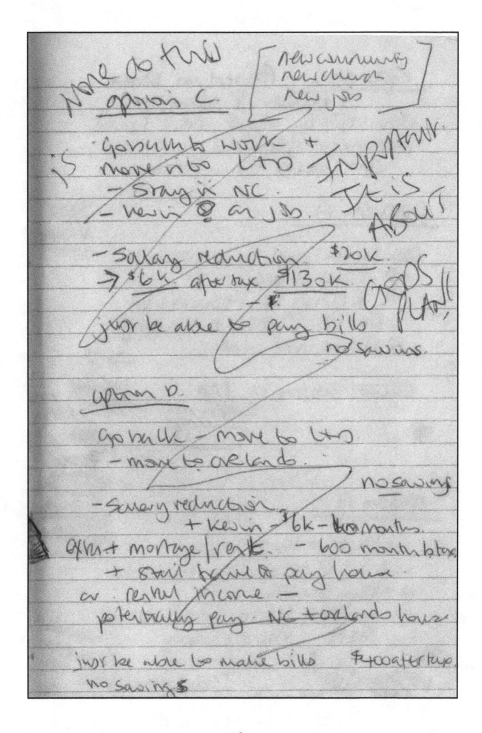

None do this
option C

[new community
new church
new job]

IS Go back to work +
move into LTD
- Stay in NC.
- Kevin @ an job.
- Salary reduction $20K.
→ $64 after tax $130K
just be able to pay bills
no savings.

IMPORTANT
It is
ABOUT
GODS
PLAN!

option D.

Go back - move to LTD
- move to orlando.
no savings
- Salary reduction
+ Kevin - 6k - two months.
rent + mortage/rent. - 600 month btax
+ still travel to pay home
or rental income -
potentially pay NC + orlando house
just be able to make bills $400 after tax
no savings

The following pages were written while I was in the 'resort'

Elaine, you know your issue - its important to take baby steps - and trust in me so that I can work through you and ~~word~~ you you can have my strength. Its important that you don't give up - don't go on The meds. Take baby steps and follow The rules and then you will be close to get out of here - small choices and know The you can do it

Don't try more/different meds - its about your inside the best psychiatrist is Jesus who lives inside of you. Snacks at 9pm

Imagine doing each day just take one day at a time - go spend time with Jesus.

Need to eat and bathe and look after yourself - the only way out of here

Elaine, you don't need to be taking
meds
psychiatry is best for yourself –
for Zeus to be working in and
through you,
Drugs is not the answer– follow
the rules –
Next steps!
→ baby steps, to get outside.

Dear Elaine do you <u>Trust me</u>
really, really trust me – Yes thank you
Jesus for the honesty.
So what next Elaine – do you Trust
me with the rest of your life? – Yes I do
lord.
So what about your job?? I have
no idea lord – well I know that
You will see me through this –
I have been battling against you
dear lord and not surrendering

I do fully surrender to You Lord
with my life and with my jobs and
with my finances and everything Lord—
I am no longer fighting against you Lord
I am here fully surrendered I have
no idea what the future holds— I know
that You hold the future Lord
My spirit is rested and I know fully
now that I am Yours Jesus.
What do we need to do to get you well
there — It's safe here Wait until
You get back on the outside — Yes Lord
it is going to be very difficult - I know
now deep in my heart and soul and spirit
that I am giving it all to You!!
No matter what the future holds Lord
I know that You hold it.
Sterm I know that you will try to
turn this around - I am going with
the Lord, He will guide my path.
I know Lord that You are right here
beside me - and inside of me

So what does the future hold??
I have no idea lord

So thankful for you lord Y nabe
forgive me my sins - not to do
into man Thank you for the forgiveness
of my sins past, present + future.
take them to you - wipe the slate
clean No need to focus on the
past, focus on the present. For all
ok - all ok - it is!!
Not need to bring into physical
light. You have brought them
all to me know I know your
heart. It is to love me
unconditionally What you did
was ok - no worries/regrets -
its important cause You keep
focused on me. Trust me
TRUST ME, TRUST ME. NOT YOU
FLESH - I brought them to you
and You have forgiven me

Mercy and this that You are pure
in your sight - I am blameless,
I am righteous - and You are irreproachable
I am forgiven. This He told me -
You know you are forgiven by me and
you don't need more forgiveness I
appreciate You for that Lord and appreciate
that I live in the present knowing You
are mine and I am Yours - there is no
eternal consequence - I am sealed by the
Holy Spirit who live in me and through me.
I am righteous, I am blameless.
No need to say anything more.

Thank you dear Jesus for what you
did taking away my sins - past present
and future I o

I am forgiven, I am forgiven -
He forgave me of all my sins.

Dear Lord,

Thank you for your forgiveness only and not man's forgiveness. I trust you with all my heart, soul and mind, knowing that You love me unconditionally.

Much more important Grace — my forgiveness or man's — Yours Lord. So thank you that I know I am forgiven by you and You have forgiven all my sins from the East and the West — not to be remembered any more. They are wiped out and erased and forgiven.

It's ok that you told her — it needed to be brought out for healing — it's all Grace because you know that I have forgiven You anyways and because of that we are able to move forward. You don't trust in self you nor us me Your one and only true

God Lord Jesus Christ and
Holy Spirit. The Holy Spirit is
alive and well in me. All things
are made new.

Do you trust me Elaine really
trust me I do — so don't need to
to tell her anything because You
are forgiven and because of that
it is okay. You will need to
move forward from this. The
temporary relief is ok You know that
I have forgiven You and that is
all that matters Thank You Lord for
your forgiveness I don't need Laura's
approval / forgiveness or more forgiveness
to really wholly trust. Don't let this
hold you back from continuing to
trust me. Doing what is right in my
eyes is more important and because
of that Lord I am so thankful for
Your forgiveness More about how
I feel & about you trust in me

and I do trust You Lord more
than words could ever say and
my actions prove that I trust you
more than I could ever say because
you know Lord that You are
with me always. I am forgiven
for all my sins, past, present
and future – You have forgiven
them. You know it was meant to
come out. I've have to move forward
and know deep really know that
I am you too. It's not about
carnal nature it's about truly
knowing me and I truly know you
Lord and that my sins are forgiven.
You don't need theirs forgiveness, You
have my forgiveness and that's all that
matters thank You Lord for your
forgiveness I trust you so much
Lord and have always trusted You.
You don't need to know about
the sins because you are forgiven

I am forgiven. I am forgiven and
I trust you Lord with all my heart and soul
You know that you didn't need to tell
Willie because I have forgiven you
That we have because that you
know that I will continue to be yours
through to the end. I am secured by
the Holy Spirit - For the time have
ceased to question anymore. You know
that you belong to Jesus and all your
sins are forgotten, erased and forgiven
So thank you Lord for your forgiveness
I told Kevin because you had told me
Lord to bring it to the light. — You have
brought it to me and that is all that
matters and thank you Lord that now I
am able to move forward with you and
Your strength because that all matters
that really because is all that matters
You trust me and... Do you know
that you are forgiven — Yes do you
know that you are blameless — Yes

do you know that Jesus I am
Yours and You have died I belong
to Your Grant — Yes so much
hard I believe this — so much —
No I am forgiven by You Lord and
that is all that matters. No break up
with Jesus or my family.
I am redeemed, I am saved,
I am free from sin and that is
all that matters. You are forgiven
by me please and thats all that
matters. No forgiveness required by
man. That is not what's important
so it's en told again — It is and
know that you eternally belong
Jesus because of the forgiveness of
my sins and that He died and
was buried and rose again
I don't need to bring me out.
It really's between me and You God
and that's all that matters.
I can do all things through Him

my lord Jesus who saves/frees
I trust you lord more than ever and
thank you for your grace — its not
about sex or anyway like that —
its about salvation — my salvation
is sealed and I have the Holy Spirit
living in me and through me. You
are not dead. You are alive in me
I so appreciate you lord for your
forgiveness of my sins. I am not
sorry Jesus took a hold on me
anymore — I belong to Jesus — I
belong to Jesus.
I am righteous with God — and I
am in right standing with Him —
Your sins are forgiven Elaine —
No need to continue to think about or
think about the them — they are blurred
out of my memory. Thank you Lord
Jesus for forgiveness of my sins
I am forgiven by Jesus and thats
all that matters.

I am forgiven, its all well with my soul and my spirit. You know were my innermost parts.

I will not leave you nor forsake you Therefore. I am forgiven by God that's all that matters Now forgiveness needed by anyone else Think of the beautiful every relationship with Jesus presently that I am forgiven by Him. there is no condemnation for those in Christ Jesus. I am in Christ Jesus

I am learning to appreciate every moment of my life don't the dead past or the imagined future. Because I am forgiven and because Freedom I can move forward freedom from shame, freedom from hopelessness. Freedom is Jesus thats all that matters, no need to tell anyone else!!

You remember my sins no more –
thank you Jesus for this, thank you
for saving me and my soul and my spirit
Do you believe that you needed to be
when – there its on that you shot
you know that I have been forgiven sin
and it won't matter about anything else,
I am forgiven – thank you, and so
I trust you Lord from this moment.
I don't need to say anymore because
everything is forgiven. I will never
meeting up with never ... I have made
up with you Lord and I have freedom
in that.

My sins are erased and it is ok.
You still have me here and you
still have the Holy Spirit living in
you. I am sealed by the Holy Spirit
I didn't need to tell heaven and
He didn't to tell me – its not
about us. Its me about You
and thats all that matters here?

I know Lord You are my master
and hands all that matters.
I am no longer anxious about
future because I know You are in
control

~~crossed out~~

Now is not the time to lose your
Trust in me. I do trust You
Lord - I am forgiven - you
have forgiven all of my sins
and so I can rest in that peace -
the peace that surpasses all
understanding. I have not lost
You Lord nor the Jesus or the
Helps Spirit the Holy Spirit is alive
and even breathes me

Saved by Jesus life that lives
in me and through me. So no
longer am I There is no condemnation
for those in Christ Jesus

You know you are forgiven and that
you didn't need to tell Eva —
because I have already forgiven You
and that's all that matters

You have not lost me, you have
not lost anything all is good in
my spirit and my soul and mind
NO! NO! NO! NO! NO! I am forgiven
and that's all that matters

Just dwell in Jesus for today —
the present moment. Know that
I have forgiven You — it's all good!

Thank you for your gift o dear Lord
gift of God in eternal life in Christ
Jesus —

I am forgiven. I can do all
things through Christ who
strengthens me

I am forgiven — Lord you remember
my sins no more!!

Fri Aug 1

Today is a new day.
Committed to getting healthy and
back to living
What has been good so far? What
learned?
- learned different coping mechanisms.
- relaxation, breathing, importance
of community, listening to other
peoples stories
- I am so thankful Lord for You
as my saviour and for taking me out
of the pit.
- Thank you for doctors & therapists
that you have provided skills and
knowledge to move on
- Thank you for the gift of life
- I am going to stay alive for me -
for my God, my husband and daughter
/ Today be committed to the meds
and coping strategies, take away
thoughts -
/ Pick up a book and read - any book.

TRUST

options? Pet Training
   " Go back to school - fill in application
   " starbucks ?

I choose life!!

I can reinvent myself

Meditate / relax
Valuable / worthy / blameless / irreproachable
start to read.
Other peoples stories are realistic and
encouraging - have the will to live.
What different ?
   Coping strategies - read
       - Olga
  prep for the ← Cruise →
      - listen music
     - Holy Yoga
Organise Sunday school paper work
be prepared ahead of time

<u>Monday Aug 11</u> ~ Happy Birthday Gordon!!

What is this all about? Frauke, only
You can change your thinking!!
Lordy I am totally surrendered to
this process.
How can you be Grand? Lord I adore
have You.
Truth is I am Yours ~ Yes You are
mine.
Amazing Love how can it be that You
my Lord should die for me? Amazing
Love I know its true, it's my joy to
honor You in all I do and all my being
You ~ You are my King, Jesus, You are
my King.
Amazing Love how can it be that You my
King would die for me? Amazing Love
I know its true ~ it's my joy to honor You
in all I do to let me honor You.

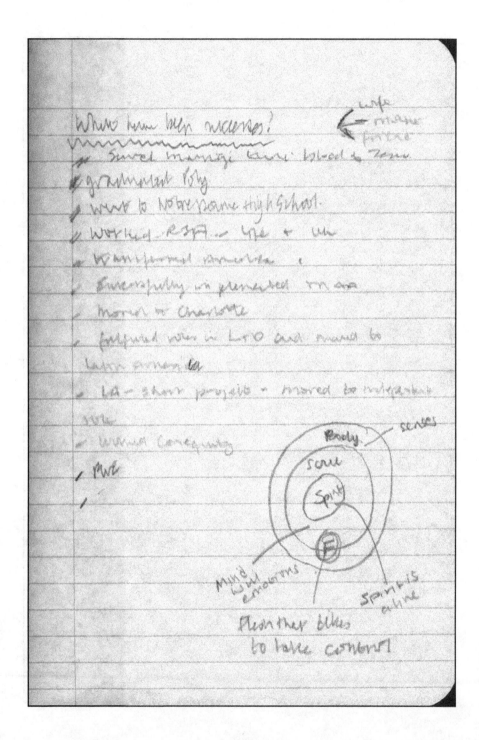

How can I go on living with ~~[illegible]~~

Elaine You can — You have not
lonely sold your soul. That is a
lie from Satan — Just can choose
not to believe the lie
You still have the Holy Spirit —
I am sealed by the Holy Spirit

Oh what do I have to be thankful for
Dear Lord — Thankful for my life, the air
that I breathe, every breath that I take
Dear Lord, thank you for turning me out as the
nurse pro. I feel like I could be so busy,
but I know you are with me dear Lord and
that it is because of You that I will be
healed
The thought of going back to work makes
me extremely anxious so Lord I have
to trust in You and remove those negative
thoughts that have built up for so long. I have
a feeling of hope somnew, but I know then

is hope in your hand, I know that I can
only do this with Your strength living in
me and through me
Focus on today and focus on the moment
Elaine Leighton 4017 Know He matters -
DOB 12/4/66
I have a chance to start again - there is a
bright future ahead - I have no idea of what it
looks like but the scary and exciting things
The future looks bright
I feel very drowsy - maybe its medication -
maybe its just this environment takes my energy

What is this breakthrough over
Jesus?
Elaine You know its because I am
with you — & You have not gone Jesus
You are with me Yes &
Jesus are you totally with me? —
Elaine. I am ——————... "I
totally with You
Elaine you can trust me — Trust Jesus
Elaine you are done with me as
Elaine you are mine — Jesus.
Jesus, Jesus, Jesus, .

What are my goals?

① To be able to walk out of this place — one foot in front of the other

② To go home and be able to communicate with friends — call them and say "Hi" and yes I had some other personal issues — but all good well without me

③ Be able to go to work full-time no idea what that looks like — it is ok

Dear Lord Jesus,
As you take me through this
journey what is it Lord –
Elaine know that I am the Almighty –
That I am your Right hand. That I
do lead you in ways seeming hidered
Elaine I am your strength.
No good or bad – it just is!"
Learn to rest in Me and in my peace.
There will be changes ahead –
see these as opportunities.

Lies — wicked
— deceitful

Truth   I am a child of god
         I am a saint
         I am the salt of the earth
         I am the light of the world.
         I am saved — which means
         I am secure in christ.
         He is my Hope
         Do you truly believe this?
         Yes — there is no way other
         than ~~you~~.
              Jesus you are the light of the
         world — You are my Hope
         If everything goes I still have you
         Jesus Yes I believe.

Songs that Have Influenced Me

Celebration – Kool and the Gang. This song is a great reminder to always be celebrating. Each moment that you are breathing is a miracle – be thankful for that.

Come Just as You Are – Crystal Lewis. This song was played the day I responded to the "altar call." A great reminder that our Lord wants us to come to Him just as we are. No need to get dressed up; simply bring our messy, imperfect selves.

Potter's Hand – Hillsong Worship. Great lyrics remind us to simply surrender to the potter and allow Him to shape and mould our lives.

Blessed Be Your Name – Matt Redman. A reminder that God is with us in the good and bad (or as I would say "not so good" times).

Not For a Moment – Meredith Andrews. This reminds me that all times God is with me, and even when I don't see, hear, or feel Him, He is always there.

Break Every Chain/Power in the Name of Jesus – The *Digital* Age. When you are lost for words, simply say one powerful word: Jesus!

Hope in Front of Me – Danny Gokey. No matter how small it seems, hang on; there is always hope.

How apt that my "go to" karaoke song of all time is

"I will survive" by Gloria Gaynor

About the Author

Originally from the UK, Elaine Sephton, aka The Real English Elaine. As a mental health advocate, she wants to raise awareness for those who seem "to have it all together", to have the courage to reach out and get the support early enough for them to experience "freedom." As a member of The National Alliance on Mental Illness (NAMI), she is inspired to build better lives for those affected by mental illness and has taken the #stigmafree pledge.

Elaine is a professional coach and holds her CHPC from the Human Potential Institute. She is a member of the ICF.

References

Angelou Maya. "Quote by Maya Angelou." GoodReads. 2020. https://www.goodreads.com/quotes/5934-i-ve-learned-that-people-will-forget-what-you-said-people.

Brown, Brené. "The Power of Vulnerability." Lecture, TED Talk. December 23, 2010. https://www.ted.com/talks/brene_brown_the_power_of_vulnerability/transcript.

Greene, Vivian. "Life isn't about waiting for the storm to pass... It's about learning to dance in the rain." Philosiblog. 2013. https://philosiblog.com/2013/07/31/life-isnt-about-waiting-for-the-storm-to-pass-its-about-learning-to-dance-in-the-rain/.

Jacobsen, Wayne. *He Loves Me! The Relationship God Has Always Wanted with You.* Newbury Park, CA: Windblown Media, 2007.

James, Allen. "Allen James." Hello Poetry. 2019. https://hellopoetry.com/AllenJames/

Meyer, Joyce. *Battlefield of the Mind.* New York : FaithWords. Revised edition, 2011.

Stanley, Charles. *The Gift of Forgiveness.* Nashville: Thomas Nelson, 1987, 1991